AF413784

Also by Bing West

Small Unit Action in Vietnam: Summer 1966

The Village

Naval Forces and Western Security

The Pepperdogs

The March Up: Taking Baghdad with the United States Marines
(with Major General Ray L. Smith)

No True Glory: A Frontline Account of the Battle for Fallujah

The Strongest Tribe: War, Politics, and the Endgame in Iraq

The Wrong War: Grit, Strategy, and the Way Out of Afghanistan

*Into the Fire: A Firsthand Account
of the Most Extraordinary Battle in the Afghan War*
(with Dakota Meyer)

One Million Steps: A Marine Platoon at War

Call Sign Chaos: Learning to Lead
(with Jim Mattis)

The Last Platoon: A Novel of the Afghanistan War

CAT 5

CAT 5

THE 2033 WAR

BING WEST

A KNOX PRESS BOOK
An Imprint of Permuted Press

Cat 5:
The 2033 War
© 2026 by Bing West
All Rights Reserved

ISBN: 979-8-89565-652-5
ISBN (eBook): 979-8-89565-653-2

Cover art by Conroy Accord

Permuted Press
New York • Nashville
permutedpress.com

Published in the United States of America
1 2 3 4 5 6 7 8 9 10

TO THE THIRTY-THREE

It was my honor to serve alongside you before you fell.

Andrew Aviles 2003

Phil Brannon 1966

Bob Butz 1965

Vince Capodanno 1968

Bill Cahir 2008

Ho Chi 1975

Will Cloney 1968

Ray Downey 2001

Paul Fielder 1966

John Fleming 1966

Glenn Foster 1969

John Glasser 1966

Tim Hetherington 2011

Rabbit Hoi 1966

Little Joe 1975

Bac Si Khoi 1973

Eric Lindstrom 2009

Frank Lummus 1969

Megan McClung 2010

Brian McPhillips 2003

Martin Medellin 2003

Joe Meyer 2016

Ron Meyer 1966

Omar 2013

Travis Patriquin 2010

Ed Smith 2003

Suong 1974

Joe Sullivan 1966

Jerry Suter 1966

Troung 1973

Phil Volentine 1968

Ken Westbrook 2009

Doug Zembiec 2007

Contents

Introduction

Like a Cat-5 hurricane gathering offshore, a two-front war—our unsustainable debt and China's rising ambition—is building toward landfall in the next decade. Its roots lie in the three wars we fought and lost. In Vietnam, Iraq, and Afghanistan, American troops won every battle; Washington lost every war. This book contrasts the grit on those battlefields with the lack of resolve inside the White House. Three defeats changed nothing.

Why didn't we win? Every war—short or long—is decided by two forces: military capability and political will. In all three conflicts, our forces had the capability. It was political will that failed. Our presidents and legislators convinced themselves that America, like Jupiter, was too powerful to lose. Even after losing, that conceit endured. Trillions were showered into entitlements even as debt ballooned. The military budget was slashed even as China surged. By examining how we failed in past wars, we can grasp the peril we now face—and prepare for the storm ahead.

"History, though based on facts, is not factual at all," Michael Oakeshott wrote. "It is a series of accepted judgments." What follows is eyewitness testimony, not an accepted secondhand judgment. I served in senior positions, but more importantly, I'm perhaps the only historian to have fought in all three wars. I was in combat alongside the grunts year after year, decade after decade. The Dedication page lists the fallen with whom I patrolled in the heat, the mud, and the dark. This book is part of their record.

Each chapter begins at the front. "The historian's task," Geoffrey Elton wrote, "is to establish what actually happened." After describing what actually happened, I turn to the policy decisions in Washington. At its core, this book contrasts how our warriors fought with how our leaders directed them.

Many volumes have dissected these wars in numbing detail. This book is short and to the point. Following Isaiah Berlin's counsel, I identify the single driving idea behind each pivotal decision. Each analysis is brief, disciplined, and focused on the decisive point.

The final chapters look ahead. By 2026, the balance of conventional military power was shifting toward China. We were falling behind in missile and drone firepower. Meanwhile, Congress had borrowed $38 trillion to expand entitlements for 200 million Americans. Politicians bought votes with debt, pushing the nation toward a fiscal cliff by 2033. Our debt and China's implacability are inseparable. For the first time in our history, we face the prospect of an economic crisis on the eve of a military challenge—before the first shot is fired. A financial, geopolitical, and constitutional collision is coming. A reckoning cannot be avoided.

Only by confronting both threats—debt and China—can we recover national purpose.

CHAPTER 1

Battle in Vietnam: Winning Hearts and Minds

The Vietnam War sneaked up on America. In 1955, communist forces drove colonialist France out of North Vietnam and infiltrated guerrillas into South Vietnam, a fledgling republic. Over the next decade, the guerrillas steadily gained control over rural areas. The American foreign policy establishment feared that if the South fell, other Southeast Asian nations would topple like a row of dominoes. Beginning in 1965, President Lyndon B. Johnson gradually and grudgingly deployed US combat units into South Vietnam.

In the spring of 1966, I arrived in Vietnam as a Marine grunt. The United States Marine Corps has been described as "the world's most lethal military force." If you are willing to fight, the Marines will pitch you into the maelstrom. I was sent to join an infantry platoon three hundred miles north of Saigon. As a twenty-six-year-old infantry captain, my job was to write a training manual about how our small units were fighting on the ground.

A month earlier, the platoon I joined had numbered fifty-two; it was down to thirty-one when I checked in. The grunts were to search for and engage the elusive VC (Vietnamese Communist) guerrillas in the rural countryside. When we stepped off on a torrid June morning, the temperature was close to one hundred degrees. Within minutes, every Marine was soaked in sweat. The scorching sun turned our three-pound steel helmets into ovens baking our heads. We plodded on, taking only measured swigs of the tepid water from our canteens, knowing the patrol had hours to go. Coherent thought became a mirage.

The flat paddies stretched in checkerboard fashion to the horizon, interspersed with thick tree lines. A grunt couldn't see beyond the next hedgerow. Navigation was by compass and guesses. The people lived in small bamboo huts with thatched roofs and dirt floors, with no electricity, running water, or sanitation. Most of the hooches were surrounded by thorn hedges to keep in the chickens, pigs, and cows. Every day, the platoon encountered snipers and mines planted on the trails, in the fields, and along the paddy dikes.

We walked in single file inside the treads of two ponderous amphibious vehicles called amtracs (boxlike troop-carrying vehicles). We were trying to avoid triggering Bouncing Betty mines. These looked like green soda cans, packed with explosives and with a spring on the bottom. Once buried, only a tiny three-prong trigger stuck up. When stepped on, the mine popped into the air, shredding legs, stomachs, and testicles.

The grunts hated the area. Our mission was to trudge along until we were shot at, then shoot back. The theory was that by patrolling, the grunts would grind down the guerrillas and protect the people. But the platoon had no translator and could not talk with the farmers. The guerrillas didn't wear uniforms, and the platoon had no way of identifying them or those providing them with shelter and food. These VC weren't part-time soldiers who toiled in the paddies by day. They were wily, full-time soldiers who fell back when they saw a heavily armed patrol. Only by sheer physical presence, by getting out and trudging along until the rounds zipped by, did the Marines have a hope of killing some of the guerrillas. There was no intel about which hamlets had ties with the VC and which hated and feared them.

When a platoon left the wire to patrol, it entered an alien world. Death lurked in the dirt, in the hooches, in the paddies, in the bush. Every step was a gamble. Sometimes you can't avoid death; you're either unlucky or outgunned. But sometimes your own fatigue blows up in your face. After several baking hours with no contact, we were passing a hamlet when—*wham!* Two quick, dull explosions, followed by a cloud of black smoke.

Three Marines were writhing in the dirt, clutching their legs. The corpsman rushed up to tie rubber tourniquets to stanch the squirting blood. Staff Sergeant William Cunningham grabbed a handset and called for a medevac helo. In frustration, he yelled at the wounded, "I told you to stay in the tracks! I told you! I told you!"

From the hamlet, rounds were snapping over our heads. We hunkered down behind a dry paddy dike as hard as concrete. Bullets were pinging off the sides of the two amtracs. One VC light machine gun and a half dozen rifles were shooting from the hamlet and from a trench line leading to a distant knoll. The medevac helo circling above us couldn't land until the platoon snuffed out the incoming fire.

A squad leader, Corporal Jerry Payne, yelled, "We're going in!" The trench line and the hamlet were three hundred meters away, a long distance under the blazing sun. Scarcely had we started forward when Payne grabbed me. "Wait! We stay in the tracks!" He waved to the two amtracs to lead the way. They chugged forward, and we followed them at a shambling trot toward the hamlet.

Before we got there, the enemy fire ceased. The Marines split up, checking one hooch after another.

"Kill them all!" a husky grunt yelled. I grabbed his pack and swung him around.

"Bullshit!" I shouted. He collected himself and we swept through fruitlessly. The women and children had fled, while the guerrillas escaped down a trench line. Assuming the trench was booby-trapped, we didn't follow.

The action had lasted less than fifteen minutes. The women cowered in a group with their children. One hooch was burning, and the crackling was the only loud sound. Sopping with sweat, the grunts flopped down. Private First Class Billy Adams had seen one guerrilla fall, but that body was dragged away. Two other bodies lay on the dusty trail, one carbine recovered. There were a few desultory, defiant shots from about a half dozen guerrillas, probably low on ammo, who had fallen back into some distant scrub growth.

We slumped down, out of water and energy. Three Marines were outbound, headed for surgery to keep their legs, God willing. The women were crying, hugging their young ones. The PFC who had screamed for blood as we raced among the hooches came up to me. In the high humidity and baking sun, his cammies were drenched.

"Sorry, sir, for losing it back there."

"No harm done," I said. "Don't repeat it."

Although we didn't know each other, what counted was that we were both grunts.

Serving in Marine infantry was a tradition in my family, beginning with my great-uncle in World War I. I was born in 1940, and my two uncles were platoon commanders in the Battle of Guadalcanal in 1942 and the Battle of Okinawa in 1945. They both made it home and shaped my youth. They filled me with Marine lore—the comradeship and the laughter, as well as tough tales of hard fighting.

My dad was a second-generation Irish Catholic, raised in a three-story tenement in South Boston. By dint of prodigious study, he graduated from Harvard Medical School, became a prominent doctor, and made sure his six children applied themselves. He checked our homework every night. His oft-repeated motto was *"Mens sana in corpore sano."*

After graduating from college at Georgetown, I was accepted at Columbia Law School. Instead, I volunteered for the Marine Corps.

My parents were more proud than surprised. They had long suspected the legacy of my uncles would kick in.

In 1963, I had drawn the weekend duty as a young lieutenant in my regiment of about three thousand Marines. That meant sleeping on a cot in the office to respond to any emergency telephone call in the middle of the night. On a whim, I visited the mess hall at four in the morning. Standing there in pressed khakis with rows of battle ribbons was our regimental commander, Colonel Brooke Nihart. He was talking with the cooks about improving the quality of the food. He knew by name all three hundred officers and senior sergeants in his command.

At every level, Marine leadership stressed the three Cs: *Competence* in your job, *Care* for those under your command, and *Conviction* in a set of standards. Nihart exhibited all three characteristics. Under his senior leadership, I commanded an infantry platoon (forty-four men) and a mortar platoon (ninety men), leaving active duty in 1965 to attend Princeton graduate school. I had always felt compelled to write, and Princeton seemed to open the right pathways.

When my regiment deployed to Vietnam, I contacted Nihart, proposing to join platoons to write a training manual for new lieutenants and sergeants. Based on his recommendation, the commandant of the Marine Corps sent me to Vietnam. So, there I was in 1966, with an exhausted platoon under a scorching sun outside a battered hamlet abandoned by the guerrillas.

With dusk settling in, we decided not to risk tripping a mine by walking back to base. We set up in a circle with clear fields of fire. The old men, women, and children abandoned their hooches and camped next to us. We didn't need an interpreter to understand their pleas and gestures. Their fear was palpable. For the Viet Cong, there were no non-combatants or civilians. The guerrillas would return and set more mines outside their hamlet. The villagers dreaded the reaction of the next American platoon after the mines struck down more Marines. They weren't staying.

With no place to go, they attached themselves to us, the innocent supplicating the strong. Cunningham radioed the company commander, who agreed that in the morning we'd escort them to a refugee camp where there were tents, food, water, and security. It wasn't a good deal; they had lost their homes and rice paddies. But it beat the alternative.

They huddled within sight of our sentries, who muttered about breaches in security. No one, though, shooed them away. One squad leader was holding the riddled black tin can of the Bouncing Betty that had cut down three of his Marines. It was a night of hurt for both sides. When a baby started to cry, the sergeant cursed, stood up, and hurled the can at the infant. Cunningham took him aside and settled him down. When the resupply helicopter came in at first light, Cunningham put the sergeant on board. He was done on the lines. He couldn't be trusted to control his emotions.

* * *

Here's a strange one. The next morning, on a main path back to base, we picked up a few fliers printed in English. The gist was that Senator J. William Fulbright, one of the few who voted against Johnson, was correct in demanding that America get out. Listen to him, the fliers urged.

By the standards of 2025, I was an incompetent grunt. Why? Because it never occurred to me to bring back a flier for the intel types. Maybe they could have driven into Da Nang, worked their local sources, and arrested the printer. There couldn't have been more than one or two shops with English type. A clever detective could trace from the shop back to the North Viet contact who knew enough from reading our newspapers to sow what is now called disinformation, a.k.a., propaganda. Okay, anyone who watched *CSI*-type TV shows would know to trace the crumbs back to their source. Back then, my tired, feeble brain connected no dots. We threw the fliers away and reported nothing about them.

* * *

I also had to learn to control myself. The next afternoon, we were harassed by a few snipers. No one was hit, but the bullets spitting by like angry bees were annoying. At twilight, we saw the sharp red winks of muzzle flashes coming from a large hooch on the far side of a dry rice paddy. We'd get scant sleep if we let that sniper keep taking shots. After taking a compass reading, I decided to go after him. Three volunteers joined me.

In full dark, we quietly approached the hooch, which had a heavy wooden door. We yelled for the occupants to come out and were met with silence. Assuming the sniper was hiding inside, I took out a grenade. The Marine behind me warned the others, "He's going to blow it!" I pulled the pin, held on to the spoon, kicked the door open, pitched in the baseball-size grenade, and ducked back.

There was a sharp *crump*, and a second later, we burst through the door. Immediately, our eyes and lungs filled with dirt, not smoke or dust, but genuine choking dirt. We couldn't see or breathe. The acrid taste of gunpower filled our mouths. We stumbled outside and waited. When there was no return fire or cries of wounded, we returned to our lines. I lay all night in my foxhole, shivering. Common sense had kicked in, and I was scared that I had killed civilians, maybe some children. At dawn, the gunny sergeant took me aside.

"Don't go back there, sir," he said. "Let it go. Let's push on."

I couldn't let it go. I went back, with the reluctant gunny and platoon trailing behind. At the hooch, the door was smashed off its hinges. Inside, an old *mama san* was sweeping grenade shards from the dirt floor. Near the family altar crouched a few little ones, staring wide-eyed at the giants. She shook her head angrily at me and resumed sweeping. Behind her was an enormous, hard-packed dirt cone that looked like a giant African anthill, with steps hacked down into a bombproof cellar. That's where the family had spent the night as the fighting swirled around their hamlet.

My knees buckled in relief. I silently thanked God. The gunny let out a long, audible sigh. It was luck that my carelessness had not ended in tragedy. From then on, when it came to firefights, part of my brain assessed not only the angles of fire but the consequences of thoughtlessness. When you fire artillery or drop bombs, you're not there to experience the results. You are at a safe emotional distance. That's not true for grunts. You see and feel your mistakes.

* * *

The next day, a grunt in the middle of the platoon column tripped a mine and five Marines were evacuated. The incoming harassing fire was moderate, and we shot back furiously until, as usual, the Viet Cong disappeared. We never knew how many we hit. After ten days of such patrols, I submitted a detailed account, stressing the tactics used by both sides. I wrote only the facts and refrained from assessing whether the patrols were achieving any mission objectives.

To my surprise, I was ordered to report to three-star Lieutenant General Lewis Walt, the commander of the one hundred thousand Marines in the northern sector of South Vietnam. I knew from briefings that Walt was fighting two wars. He had deployed half his force to combat the North Vietnamese soldiers advancing south through the jungles. In the lowland populated areas, the other half of the force was spread out in platoons like the one I had joined. In most districts, the VC had established shadow governments with civilian and military leaders. The mission of the Marine platoons was to push out the VC, allowing the villagers, in theory, to support the government. This was called "pacification."

Conversely, the top commander in Vietnam, General William Westmoreland, disapproved of using American forces for pacification. He was convinced that killing tens of thousands of NVA (North Vietnamese Army) soldiers would force the North to quit. But Westmoreland did not directly countermand the Marine commander.

With a large frame, close-cropped hair, and piercing blue eyes, Walt questioned me intensely. He held up my report, with several sentences underlined. He was troubled by its tone and the casualties taken by the platoon. His aides had warned me that he began every morning by reading the names of those killed on the prior day. My report indicated that patrolling blind, with no translator or communications with the villagers, was getting nowhere. That upset him, but he didn't reprimand me. Instead, he sent me to a different unit, with instructions to again report what I saw.

* * *

While I was with Cunningham's platoon, my colleague, Captain Buck Darling, flew with his 130-man company to rescue a recon unit. The eighteen Marines had been pinned down all night atop a scraggly hill, under assault by hundreds of North Vietnamese. The enemy pulled back, covered by a rearguard shooting from trenches and holes dug deep into the slope. Exposed to accurate fire, the Marines crawled forward, pitching grenades into one hole after another. When a sniper killed Lance Corporal Terry Redic, his platoon commander, Lieutenant Ron Meyer, wriggled forward. Nicknamed "Stump" for his stocky frame, he lobbed a grenade into a hole and turned to look upslope. A North Vietnamese popped out of the hole, shot him in the back, and ducked back down. A corpsman trying to shield his dead lieutenant was shot in the chest. Lieutenant Phil Freed, a pilot attached to the company to provide air support, called in an F-8. As the aircraft strafed not twenty yards in front of them, Corporal Sam Roth ran forward, stood over the hole, and plunged a bayonet into the sniper's back.

Mopping up on Hill 881.

The Marines lost ten on Hill 881. Darling, Meyer, and I had served in the same battalion. Now Stump was gone, Buck's company was pulled back to refit, and Walt had assigned me to another unit.

* * *

The platoon I joined next was commanded by Lieutenant Tony Monroe. His grunts liked him because he schemed to keep them alive. Tony's platoon was responsible for patrolling five square miles containing ten hamlets and about eight thousand farmers. Cunning and patient, Tony avoided patrolling at obvious times and places. In late afternoons, his troops would glass the movement of the villagers heading from the paddies back to their hamlets. When only a faint twilight was still lingering, we'd follow the trail used by the last group of villagers in single file. This minimized the chances of stepping on a mine. At some point on the trail, we'd drop off into the bush or onto a bit of high ground, spread out, lie down, and doze under a rotating guard until first light.

On most patrols, nothing happened. We'd watch mostly women bending over and over to plant thin reeds of rice, while kids lazed on the backs of massive water buffaloes tugging iron plows through the mud. Usually, no armed enemy appeared. When they did, the results were mediocre or nothing at all. Situation reports were recorded only when engagements lasted longer than a brief flurry of shots.

On one occasion, we were lying all day on a parched hillside under a broiling sun. In a valley a half mile away, small groups of guerrillas carrying AK-47s and carbines were wandering about, some chatting with the women in the paddies, while others filled their canteens at a small spring. What impressed me was the close, casual contact between the guerrillas and the farmers. No wonder mines were daily set in everywhere we were apt to walk.

Tony called artillery down on a band of four. One shell after another was adjusted to no avail. The guerrillas knew they were out of our rifle range and ignored the absurdly inaccurate artillery. I ran out of water and was cramping up with a wicked headache. Tony gave me his canteen, saving me from heat stroke.

Lieutenant Tony Monroe.

Desperate for water, we formed a skirmish line and swarmed downhill to seize that spring. The surprised VC backed off into the bush, shooting sporadically. We plopped iodine tablets into our canteens now full of dirty water and headed back to our encampment. I placed two full canteens attached to my cartridge belt on my shoulders and turned to speak to Tony. There was a buzzing sound like a bee as a small caliber bullet passed through the small open space between us. We joked that the sniper had been thrown off his sight picture by seeing four heads on two bodies.

Our camp consisted of fox holes and depressions scooped out of the dirt under the shade of palm trees, with a trench latrine. I visited the latrine and lazily ambled back across an open area. *Wham!* someone hit me across the back with a baseball bat, knocking me on my face. A bullet had glanced off the back of my helmet, smacking me to earth. I lay dazed for a second, then scrambled up and sprinted to the trees, where several wide-eyed Marines were clustered.

The gunny sergeant grabbed me. "Holy shit, sir! We thought you were dead."

⁕ ⁕ ⁕

The high command next sent me to a company (140 troops) occupying a hamlet called Thanh My Trung. When the Marines had arrived a month ago, they found English-language leaflets on the trails, urging them to protest the war. The children would not return waves, the villagers hid in their hooches, and the school was closed. In the week I spent there, not one shot was fired and no mines were found. Day and night, the company was throwing out patrols that encountered only leeches. When I stripped down after one six-hour patrol, I burned off a dozen of the bloodsuckers. The village chief had moved back into his own hooch. Several times during the week, he invited elders from adjoining hamlets to join him in meeting with Captain Jim Cooper, who handed out cigars and peaches from our C-rations. The children obeyed Gunny Sergeant Jack Montera's rule to line up by age—youngest first—for a daily candy treat after school.

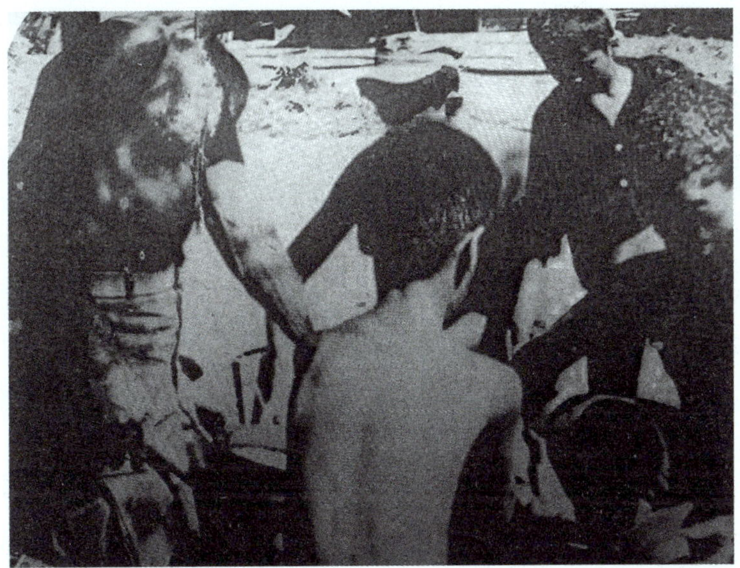

Gunny Sergeant Jack Montera.

Inside the hamlet, the Marines strolled casually about. They seemed accepted. But it couldn't last. The Thanh My Trung hamlet numbered six thousand villagers. The Marines would need 300,000 troops to station a company in each hamlet. The math, called troop-to-task ratio, did not add up. When Cooper's company was pulled out, the hamlet chief moved to a hillside fort held by a local-government force. The Viet Cong moved back into Thanh My Trung without firing a shot.

* * *

Not having enough Marines, Walt tested an economical approach—deploying a handful of grunts into each village. He sent me to an isolated village called Binh Nghia ("Just Cause"), with a population of five thousand farmers. Two weeks before I arrived, a squad of fifteen Marines had moved in. The district chief, in charge of fifty such villages, had assured the Marine command that most farmers didn't like the VC, but were terrified of them. A militia unit called Popular

Forces (PFs), led by Suong, was supposed to guard the village. The PFs were untrained farmers paid nineteen dollars a month. They huddled inside their small fort whenever the Viet Cong entered the village.

The village was divided into six hamlets, each holding a few hundred hooches made of laced bamboo slats, with bamboo windows and roofs of thick thatch. The floors were packed earth, with wooden beds separated by a thin screen from the main room, with an ancestral altar and a cooking fire. Hundreds of banana and palm trees with broad leaves sheltered the hamlets from the harsh sun.

When I arrived, the Marines were living in a white, one-room schoolhouse called Fort Page, named for a Marine killed on the path leading to the fort. The Marines, PFs, and village officials slept on cots in a canvas tent, with water from a deep well. A single coil of barbed wire and a shallow ditch ringed the fort's small perimeter, supplemented by rows of short, sharpened stakes called punjis, and a rickety bamboo fence supposed to deflect rocket grenades. The scrawny fort looked like it was built from tinker toys.

Fort Page, 1966.

On the other side of the river, less than a half mile away, lay the Phu Long hamlets, home of the aggressive P-31st Viet Cong company that had bragged they would massacre the Americans. Crossing at night in concave basket-like boats, they collected taxes, held indoctrination meetings, met with relatives and girlfriends, and left before dawn.

Sergeant Joe Sullivan welcomed me as an added rifleman. At twilight, I joined three Marines and three PFs in the fort's courtyard. The PFs, dressed shabbily and toting World War II rifles, jabbered nervously. If one were killed, his family was left with nothing. Each Marine carried two hundred rounds for his heavy M-14 rifle and four to six grenades. To avoid making noise, no one wore a helmet or an armored vest. Lacking a radio, we set out with only a few red flares to shoot off if we were pinned down. In single file, we silently moved up the dirt trail, with dark hooches on both sides.

A clattering began, the thwacking of sticks against the hollow core of heavy bamboo staves. It was like listening to children playing with drums, without style, syncopation, or melody, just cacophony. When we turned toward the sound, that signaler ceased, and farther on, another picked up, trying to frighten us with noise. Warriors have done that for ten thousand years, shaking spears, hurling oaths, pounding on shields.

We pushed on until we reached a tangle of brush blocking the trail, a signal that the VC were inside the hamlet. Heeding the warning, the PFs balked. Corporal Phil Brannon was having none of it. He grabbed a PF and pulled him forward. We pushed ahead and soon were in a blind firefight. Neither side could see the other. Our tracers were red and theirs were green. We'd fire a burst of bullets in a red stream and roll away before a stream of green came back. Unable to close in on us, the enemy slipped away after about twenty minutes. None of us was foolish enough to venture forward into the kill zone to check for bodies.

The next morning, the farmers were out again plucking rice or fishing. The children were in school, and the Marines were greeted warmly, as though nothing had happened the night before. I ate duck eggs and peanuts, drank coconut juice, and wandered around like a curious tourist. Everywhere, I encountered smiles.

This continued night after night. When dusk came, so did the guerrillas. At twilight, six or eight PFs and Marines would leave the fort. Watchers for the guerrillas would beat out on bamboo poles. Villagers in their hooches would blow out their candles. In the dark, we walked slowly and silently. Our advantage was that we could pitch grenades forty yards, much farther than the Viets. If we received too much fire, we'd crawl away. The VC did the same.

The firefights were testing encounters. In a brief night fight, four or five of us would each send a hundred heavy 7.62-mm rounds down range, pitching grenades and popping off a few light antiarmor explosives and a dozen M-79 shells the size of a small hand grenade. That's a heavy dose of metal tearing up the dirt, plants, leaves, trees, and bodies of any guerrillas who hadn't crawled away.

One moonlit night, I was lying in ambush with Lieutenant Tom O'Rourke and a half dozen others. I spotted two guerrillas sneaking across a dry paddy to throw grenades at us. As I straightened the pin to pitch my grenade, Tom shook his head and gestured at his rifle. Easy shot. Stubbornly, I ignored him, stood up, and heaved my grenade. It sailed over the heads of the enemy and exploded. In the ensuing smoke, both escaped, setting a world record for the hundred-yard dash.

Tom wouldn't speak to me for a day. Brannon, a sharpshooter from west Texas, was amused. I hadn't sensibly used my rifle, and I spoke with a peculiar accent. "My new job," he joked, "is to get our captain home to Boston in one piece, so he can go to Haavaad Yaad."

The skirmishes didn't slack off. *Bang, bang, bang.* That's all we did, night after night, exchange bursts in the pitch black and then both sides pull back. The battalion command center usually came up on the net back at the fort, demanding a body count. No one was idiotic enough to go forward and risk what might follow.

What was driving this constant contact? A local feud. The chief of Phu Long village across the river was Le Quan Viet, the one-armed leader of the P-31st VC company. For a year, he had extorted rice and taxes from Binh Nghia, and the villagers attended "teaching sessions" in the marketplace. Then the Marines came, and the Viet Cong couldn't enter without resistance. But they kept trying, night after night, while the PFs gradually gained in skill and confidence.

Father Vince Capodanno, a chaplain, visited us one hot afternoon. He didn't rate a helicopter, so he had driven six miles over mine-infested back roads to visit us. He chatted with each grunt, said a short mass, and departed. He later died sheltering a wounded grunt and was awarded the Medal of Honor.

Not knowing the village routine, we missed opportunities. One night we walked past a long dhow tied up to a rickety dock. Under lanterns, laborers were walking up the gangplank with sacks of rice. They stopped and stared at us. Our farmers/PFs fidgeted but said not a word. We moved on and set in a few hundred meters upstream. Within minutes, green tracers were arcing in, spraying our position as the dhow drifted away downstream with the current. We had stumbled upon a supply boat for the North Vietnamese soldiers hiding back in the mountains, and the farmers/PFs were too frightened to tell us.

* * *

The bravest man I never knew came close to killing me one sweltering night. We had set in an ambush on the bank of the Tra Bong river. Around midnight, a towering storm rolled in from the mountains to the west. We lay drenched amid booming thunder and flashes of lightning. One bolt struck so close that in the burst of brilliant light, I saw a man standing erect in a bamboo basket boat poling past us, not twenty feet from the bank. I nudged my four companions to go flat. Sure enough, seconds later we heard the telltale *ping!* of a grenade spoon. The mud and water muffled the explosion and flattened the shrapnel, and no one was injured. In response, our heavy bullets ripped up the shrubs where the man was hiding. He had acted with amazing courage. Of course, we didn't go into the bush searching for him, but it's doubtful he survived our fusillade.

* * *

After weeks of continuous night fights, we said the usual good-byes, including about staying in touch, and I moved on to another unit. Three weeks later, the P-31st Viet Cong company, more than a hundred strong, attacked at midnight in a slight drizzle. Of the seventeen Marines and PFs in the photo below, nine were killed. In one blow, the Combined Action Platoon (CAP) had lost its sergeant and half its men.

That was hard; I knew every one of them. We had shared many sopping, mosquito-bitten ambushes together. I stayed in touch with their families for years. In the picture on the following page, Brannon is wearing the beret, and Sullivan is to his left.

Standing from left: *John Glasser, killed; Culver, wounded; Garcia, wounded; Thielipape, wounded; Jerry Suter, killed; John Fleming, killed; Learch, wounded; Carlson, Wingrove, Brannon, killed; Joe Sullivan, killed. Kneeling: Pham, killed; Trong, killed; Hoai, killed; Swinford, Melton, Fieldler, killed.*

There was nothing special about the grunts at Fort Page. They were Marines with a shared spirit and culture. Following just two decades after World War II, there was an unspoken assumption throughout the infantry that death would come. When the general suggested that the survivors could pull out if they wanted, they reacted angrily. They had lost too many to give up.

The volunteers who replaced the fallen were led by Sergeant Jim White. Raised on a horse farm, Jim had a muscular frame and an easy smile. The night patrols continued at the same pace, with roaming listening posts added so that a large enemy force could not again gather unnoticed. The Americans' angry response to losing spilled over onto the PFs. After four months, they were fairly well-trained and knew they were marked. When the Marines persisted in going out, the PFs accompanied them and did not run away, as they had in June.

The grunts never called for artillery or air support inside the village, because they lived there. The villagers welcomed them into their thatched homes. One day, Corporal Larry Wingrove saw a farmer lashing out at a whimpering ten-year-old boy. Angered, Wingrove stepped in. He brought the boy to the fort when he learned that the boy was an orphan no one cared for. Dubbed "Little Joe," the boy lived happily with the CAP Marines. After the US withdrew from Vietnam, he was shot and killed.

Author and Little Joe in Binh Nghia Village.

I was with the Marines in the village on New Year's Day in 1967. To celebrate the holiday, Jim finagled the loan of a movie screen and projector. Thousands of villagers packed the marketplace to watch *Breakfast at Tiffany's*, with the women demanding rewinds to exclaim about the apartments in the Big Apple.

Later, the village chief, Trao, wrote this letter to Jim's parents:

"Sgt. White and his Sq. (squad) evry days evry night go to empust with P.F.... They work very hard and never look tired.... My people are very poor and when to see a marine they are very happy.... P.F. and marine to fight V.C. Maybe die.... Jod bless you all.[1]

Ho Chi, the village schoolteacher, added his sentiments to the letter:

"To Sgt. White Family...I hope in my heart that Sgt. White does come back when my country is at peace. Many of my American friends have died. I'm very sorry at has happened to your people. I hope someday we will all have peace and Charity. Your friend always, Ho Chi."

After I wrote my report, I met with Walt and his operations officer, Colonel John Chaisson, a Harvard graduate from Boston with an inquiring mind. They decided that placing squads in the villages yielded more security with less manpower than stationing companies on the surrounding hills. However, adopting the CAP would not be mandated from the top. Each battalion commander, coordinating with the local district chief, would decide which villages were appropriate. Some battalion commanders deployed squads into villages and some did not. The CAP concept remained a localized tactic, not a strategy applied everywhere.

CHAPTER 2

Battle in Vietnam:
Search and Destroy

Colonel John Chaisson decided I had seen enough of the pacification/counterinsurgency war. It was time for me to report on the "main force war," the "search and destroy" efforts by US battalions (there are around eight hundred soldiers in a battalion) to engage the NVA battalions in the jungles.

Chaisson first sent me to the Demilitarized Zone at the northern tip of South Vietnam. The DMZ, lugubriously dubbed the Dead Marine Zone, stretched from the South China Sea thirty miles west to the thick jungles of Laos. In 1966, one hundred thousand NVA soldiers marched through Laos to invade South Vietnam. Some units walked south three hundred miles to reach positions opposite Saigon. Others set up base camps in the highlands at the center of the country. The largest force took the shortest route, swarming directly across the DMZ to fight the Marines who held the northernmost of South Vietnam's four military corps. The top North Vietnamese general, Vo Nguyen Giap, boasted, "I have the American Marines stretched taut as a bow string, and I will break them."

I joined a Force Recon company based on an outcropping called the Rockpile, north of the lone road leading into Laos. The recon's job was to send out tiny scouting parties. After a few shakedown patrols to check my competence, I joined a five-man team. Our mission was to insert ten miles inside the DMZ to locate NVA main forces. At the takeoff zone, one grunt began to vomit and had to be left behind. Taking his radio, I replaced him. In predawn darkness, the five of us flew by helicopter at treetop level for several miles, dipping in and out of valleys to confuse the enemy about where we were landing. Just before dawn, we hopped out in a small clearing near the Ben Hai River separating North from South Vietnam.

We slipped under the jungle canopy that we called the bush. We spent all day walking silently along the slopes of the thick hillsides, avoiding both the ridgelines and the valley floors. Sometimes the slopes were so steep that we had to cling to vines to avoid falling. Slipping sideways hour after hour, we edged along where no sane man would walk, minimizing the chance we'd bump into enemy soldiers. We didn't have night-vision devices, didn't wear helmets or armored vests, and navigated by placing a compass on top of a map. We heard the enemy often, chopping wood and yelling back and forth. Late on the first afternoon, we smelled them. The North Vietnamese ate rice laced with dried fish. The odor drifted up from the valley floor. (Captured North Vietnamese said we smelled like the discarded skins of snakes.)

We slept that night inside tangles of brush and thorns. Without talking, we ate uncooked C-rations. I was partial to the peaches and fruit cocktail; no one ate the ham and lima beans. No one even thought of smoking a cigarette or coughing.

We ran out of canteen water on the second day and couldn't find a stream bed to refill. The heat was sapping us, and I had a splitting headache. The second afternoon, looking down from a knoll, we saw a dozen North Viets in clean khakis crossing a bamboo footbridge behind a guide dressed in loose blue pajamas. They were yapping and laughing, without weapons. Conclusion: We found a base camp.

It rained that night, and we slept restlessly in the brambles. My treasure was a green T-shirt wrapped in plastic. Each night, I shrugged out of my sopping bush shirt and slipped on the dry T-shirt. Pretty soon, however, the damned rain had soaked it. At first light, we crawled back to our vantage point. A mist covered the stream, but we heard them coming awake, their sing-song voices sounding like birds chirping. We called for artillery fire, saying we heard voices in a streambed. Back at the gun tubes, the fire coordinator labeled the target as "talking fish."

The first salvo rippled into the dense foliage, and a few soldiers ran across the bridge, returning with bamboo poles wrapped with bundles of white bandages. We called for more fire and a dozen NVA splashed across the stream. We jacked up our next radio call, estimating one hundred enemies. Shells started pounding in. The bridge was blown apart and bodies drifted downstream. More than four hundred shells rained down in half an hour.

The NVA got it together, and figured out where we were. When dozens of them swarmed up the slope to our front, we ran down the other side. We came to a dry stream bed and bounded down like rabbits from one large boulder to another. I was thinking that if one of us broke a leg, we were finished. When we reached the bottom, we looked for undergrowth in which to hide. No luck; the valley floor was covered only with knee-high wilted grass. We were winded, with no place to go.

Back in the rear, the operations officer had sent a small, one-engine Air Force spotter plane to check things out. The pilot saw us and fired a single, red rocket at the enemy on the hill above us.

"Get your heads down," he radioed.

I was angry and disappointed. One two-foot rocket? That was all the help we were getting? The next moment, the world exploded. The earth bounced, and tree trunks and boulders flew over our heads. Only later were we told that a Marine F-8 jet had been flying north to bomb a bridge. The pilot in the spotter plane radioed the F-8 pilot that we were going under and to drop both his two-thousand-pound bombs. The spotter rocket burst open about three hundred meters away. Those four thousand pounds of high explosives sheared off the top of the hill behind us, shattering all pursuit.

Parched and exhausted, we stumbled across the open field and hid in the jungle. Several hours went by before enemy search parties came, shouting back and forth. They had no chance of finding us. We were snuggled so deep in the bush that we could scarcely see each other. The spotter pilot estimated fifty bodies strewn along the stream and the gouged-out hillside. Headquarters called, telling us to sneak back to confirm the count. More were likely killed by the two-thousand-pound bombs. Attached is the official debrief I received many years later.[1] We stayed right where we were, ignoring the call to commit suicide. With the enemy all around, no chopper could land during daylight. We slept fitfully and a helo plucked us out before dawn on the next day.

The pilot, Major Orson Swindle, was shot down a few weeks later. He was captured and served six torturous years in the Hanoi prison. Decades after his release, we met so that I could thank him. Thinking he had killed us, he said his happiest moment was when we recovered our senses and cursed over the PRC radio. His cellmate as a prisoner of war was John McCain, who later became a senator. When McCain ran for president in 2008, Swindle delivered the nominating speech.

All those unsuspecting enemies killed, and we hadn't fired one bullet. We watched the enemy scurrying, and through our PRC-25 radio, adjusted the arty that scythed down some, while Swindle's bombs obliterated the others who were chasing us. It wasn't personal, five killing fifty. We saw them falling but heard few screams, just the thudding of the arty rounds. We never saw Swindle's F-8. When I reported to Lieutenant General Lewis Walt and Chaisson, I explained how the five of us had used artillery and air to attack. We were, in essence, a bomber pilot in a plane that never left the ground.

To quote the official Marine history, "They [Walt and Chaisson] expressed the opinion that such missions deserved a special section in the reporting system and selected the name Operation Stingray. The marriage of the reconnaissance Marines and artillery was one of the major innovations of the war."[2] Between 1966 and 1972, Operation Stingray teams inflicted more than twenty thousand fatalities upon the enemy.

* * *

Sergeant Orest Bishko was a stalwart patrol leader. He was a hunter who persisted in stalking the enemy even when we were exhausted. Six decades later, his memory lived on, attested by this email I received in July of 2025.

From: n.galadza@gmail.com

Hello Sir,

I've never forgotten July 26–29, 1966, since reading about my uncle, Orest Bishko, and the patrol you led. Now, working with troops on Ukraine's front lines, 'Brothers in Arms' means more than ever.

One of our drone crews named a large recon/bomber 'Bayda's Back' after him. 'Bayda'—a historic Ukrainian kozak— was known for his fierce spirit. My uncle was always 'Bayda' to our family. Somewhere on the Eastern Front, one of your brothers still fights for freedom.

Ever grateful,

Nikolai Galadza

Of course, I was touched—flabbergasted, really—to receive that email. The warrior's spirit had burned in Sgt. Bishko in Vietnam. And it burned in his nephew half a century later. The Ukrainians were fighting for their existence. We shouldn't fight their war for them. But neither should we, nor other wealthy European democracies, deny them the arms to fight with all their might to remain free.

* * *

Chaisson next sent me to two battalions—designated 1/5 and 2/5—spread out to fight the NVA where the hills sloped down to the paddies. I checked in at the 2/5 support base on a burning hot day in July 1966. The line companies were out on sweeps. I was walking by the helo pad when a shot-up H-34 helicopter fluttered down, with the pilot yelling that a chopper was down. As the nearest officer, I grabbed six Marines as a rescue party. The helo climbed to three thousand feet, where cooler air felt bracing. Ugly yellow smoke was spiraling from a paddy, and within seconds, the pilot had plopped us next to the burning chopper. We grabbed the crew and struggled out of the paddy, with bullets splashing around us.

Once tucked behind a paddy dike, I took compass headings on two peaks and radioed our location. Within an hour, two hundred Marines were moving upslope, harassed by desultory shots. We entered a small hamlet tucked under the broad leaves of the jungle canopy. I wandered into a tidy, one-room hooch where soup was on the hearth, bananas on the table, and a child's schoolbook open to a crude drawing of a stick figure firing at a helicopter.

A thunderstorm swept over us, and out of water and out of brains, I stood under a thatched roof and guzzled down a stream of raindrops. The thatch contained the feces of farm animals, including water buffalo. Over the next three decades, parasites nibbled at my stomach lining until my intestines occasionally ballooned out under my skin. My daughter commented that it looked gross. It took three operations to stitch my stomach together again.

When the rain let up, the lieutenant colonel began pulling his troops back to the valley floor. He asked me to go back to higher headquarters to confirm where we were. As we flew out, I watched our jets dropping napalm on the hillside. The crew chief thought I would be pleased. I was saddened, thinking of the crayon drawing by a child somewhere down there.

Entering the headquarters tent ten miles in the rear, I pointed to a map and tapped the center of a grid square with red hash lines. The colonel exploded. "I talked to General Westmoreland personally!"

he yelled. "A dozen B-52s from Guam are already in the air. Now I have to call them off because your unit's in their drop zone!"

It seemed appropriate to exit and sleep fitfully under a drizzle, with the 105 howitzers pounding away at a dark jungle.

*　*　*

The next afternoon, I joined Lieutenant Tony Monroe's platoon in a three-hour movement at dusk to set up an ambush outside a hamlet. As planned, a tank noisily moved toward the hamlet at dawn, and a dozen NVA in khaki uniforms bolted from the hooches. Following a guide in black pajamas, they ran down a path in single file. Seeing us two hundred yards to their front, they darted into a waist-high field of dry corn stalks and lay down. We advanced on line to spray the field. They had no escape.

Suddenly, there was a sharp *crack!* and two blinding flashes a hundred yards in front of us. We hit the ground as shrapnel zinged over our heads. The battalion commander, watching from a faraway knoll, had called in an artillery strike. We had almost become part of the 10 percent of our troops killed by friendly fire. Tony was furious at his callous commander.

I hitched a ride out to write up my notes, while the battalion resumed its sweep. With no vehicles, they moved in a Y formation, following compass headings on an inaccurate map. As they passed small hamlets, sniper fire from the tree lines increased as the civilians fled. Regardless of whether you are in Vietnam or fifty years later in Iraq or Afghanistan, when the villagers leave, the ambush begins.

In the sweltering afternoon heat, Company A bumped into a dozen enemy soldiers shooting from the far side of the rice paddies. Marines splashing across a paddy were pinned down, lashed by enfilade fire. A heavy squall swept in from the mountains, preventing supporting fires. Five were killed, while others crawled to the shelter of the paddy dike. As PFC Larry Bailey later described, "They were everywhere, in the banana trees, behind the dikes and in the paddies."

Captain Jim Furleigh, commanding A Company, rushed up another squad. Lieutenant Buck Darling brought up Bravo Company. Bands of ten to twenty North Viets were darting back and forth about a hundred meters to their front, probing by fire for gaps in the front. Finding none, the NVA dropped into trench lines dug into the soft mud. The small Viets crouched and fired across the paddies at knee level. Lying prone, the grunts returned the fire. With neither side able to advance, the ambush became a fight between two hedgehogs. Three hours into the fight, the Viets were running out of ammo. Their outgoing fire slackened.

On the Marine side, helicopters were flaring in among sheets of rain to drop off ammo and fly out the wounded. Two A-4 jets skimmed across the battlefield, not dropping any bombs. Their noise on repeated runs forced the Viets to cease firing and duck. Each time, the Marines bounded forward five or ten yards.

Lieutenant Art Blades of Bravo Company was pushing forward with his platoon, unable to see twenty meters amid the under-growth. His lead squad paused at a small opening, and from thirty feet away, withering fire killed three of them and wounded another three. Lance Corporal Irwin Brazzel led three grunts forward in a dash. All were cut down, writhing from their wounds. A corpsman stood up and was killed. Three engineers crawled forward to Brazzel and kept him alive.

Blades was in anguish. His platoon was decimated, and he hadn't seen a single enemy. Two Marines crawled up next to him. "Use grenades," Blades said. In response, they offered him several grenades. "Do I look like John Wayne?" Blades yelled. "Throw your own grenades!" The Marines kept crawling forward, pitching grenades.

Only occasionally did they glimpse a head or a hand, but the enemy's fire was slackening. Blades carefully got to one knee. He had reached the end of the trench. The shooting had sputtered out. He limped to the trench and looked down. It was clogged with nineteen bodies. The blood had gushed out, deflating them. When I arrived in late afternoon, they looked like oversized dolls, not full-grown men. The green-headed flies were everywhere, and the stench was growing. Blades ordered his reluctant grunts to fill in the trench.

In three hours, fourteen Marines had been killed. The North Viets lost fifty or sixty. This was General William Westmoreland's strategy of "search and destroy." Americans searched until the North Viets stopped evading and dug in to fight.

*　*　*

That night, we spread out under a stand of palm trees. Having commanded a mortar platoon, digging in under a prominent terrain feature seemed crazy, but not to Tony's battalion commander. The mortars hit us at midnight, the shells dropping straight down with a sound like ripping apart a newspaper. One wounded Marine kept screaming for his mother, while others tried do shush him. At dawn, I snapped a picture of Marines carrying a body in a poncho.

I knew most of the men in the platoon. "Who is he?" I asked. No one knew him. He was a replacement who had hopped off a re-supply chopper the previous evening. Only his dog tag held his name. He was dead ten hours later, with no one likely to write to his parents. A helicopter took away the body and we continued the sweep. We were fighting in the six-

No one knew him.

ties, a short time after World War II, when thousands of Marines died storming islands like Iwo Jima. You focused on the mission. No pause, no farewell to the fallen.

Jim Furleigh the company commander, and I trailed after the point squad. We hadn't advanced a klick under sniper fire when we saw a large house with a thatch roof surrounded by emerald green paddies.

Why was it still standing, attractive and untouched? Curious, we went inside. An old couple greeted us, smiling and bowing. No, they had seen no enemy. Of course not. We thanked them and left. Jim opened the rear gate. *Blam!* In a flash of white light, I was knocked backward, never hearing the explosion. Jim was gushing blood. The corpsman quickly stanched his wounds while calling a medevac. His eventual recovery would take months. I had only scratches and a piercing echo in my ears.

In the courtyard, the elderly couple were crying and holding each other, their house stood etched against the blue sky behind them.

The booby-trapped house.

"Burn it," I ordered.

On the way out, we stumbled upon two heavy-spring bear traps, usually set to wound a tiger stalking the buffs. We found a wooden crossbow and a cluster of bamboo poles sharpened like spears, plus rice mounds hidden under banana leaves. What more did I need to see to get it? For whatever reason—fear or loyalty—the locals were working with the North Viets. The old couple fearfully clinging together had not warned us. Yes, had they done so, they might later have been beheaded. That wasn't my business. I didn't want another Jim Furleigh walking in. The house went up in flames.

* * *

For months, General Walt and Colonel Chaisson had sent me across the extensive battlefields. Walt was fighting two wars. Full-scale battalion operations like Jim Furleigh's were called "search and destroy." The top commander in Vietnam, Army General William Westmoreland, believed that killing ("destroying") tens of thousands of NVA soldiers would force the North to quit. Walt had deployed half his force to such search-and-destroy missions deep inside the jungles.

Westmoreland wanted to leave it to the South Vietnamese army and PFs to destroy the Viet Cong guerrillas and its political infrastructure nestled inside the rural farmlands. Walt respectfully disagreed. He employed the other half of his force to counterinsurgency in the populated lowlands. This included CAPs like Sgt. Sullivan's in the village of Binh Nghia and companies like Capt. Jim Cooper's in Thanh My Trung.

* * *

When I got back to the States, I compiled my combat narratives into a training manual entitled *Small Unit Action in Vietnam*. In sixty thousand words that described nine actions, the short book explained both types of combat—counterinsurgency and search and destroy. The focus was upon the details that mattered to sergeants and lieutenants. Keep your head on a swivel, watch where you step, trace your location on a map, keep supporting arms on call, expect contact, and don't turn aside for the casualties. Your first job is to establish fire superiority. Keep your honor clean, but trust no one. I described how to stay alive and kill the enemy. I didn't address strategic objectives or rationales.

Training manual written by the author.

* * *

In 1967, Walt went home and Colonel Chaisson was promoted to brigadier general (one star). He was sent to Saigon to serve under four-star General Westmoreland as Director of Current Operations. While Chaisson was loyal to his boss, he disagreed with the strategy of search and destroy, restricted to South Vietnamese territory. We couldn't pursue the enemy, who, when hard-pressed, could cross back into Laos or North Vietnam to rest and refit. Chaisson believed it was crazy to concede the initiative. With Hanoi constantly sending its young men south to do battle, American soldiers and Marines had to fight them on the defense.

When I returned in the fall of 1967, he sent me back to the DMZ, where the fighting was fiercest. A year earlier up there, I had gone deep into the bush on Sgt. Bishko's Force Recon team. This time, Chaisson wanted a report on the big fights, where thousand-man battalions were slugging it out. In early fall, I flew to a twisted, soggy hilltop called Con Thien, or "Hill of Angels." More accurately, it was "Morgue of the Dead." The front looked like World War I, a smoke-smeared sky, viscous mud, broken strands of barbed wire, saggy sandbagged bunkers, filthy troops, and the constant crackle of distant small arms fire mixed with the sharp crack of incoming shells.

Con Thien was only five miles south of the Ben Hai River, which separated North from South Vietnam. Thousands of the enemy surged across the river to launch attacks, then retreated to the far bank, with US troops forbidden to give chase. Instead, Westmoreland ordered the southern half of the DMZ cleared and held. This was exactly what North Vietnam's top commander, General Giap, wanted. The DMZ was the natural restricted ground upon which to grind down the Americans. Westmoreland repeatedly expressed his personal frustration to the mud-splattered grunts. But each time, he strode to his helicopter and returned to his regal perch in Saigon. Am I angry today about generals who know their orders are deeply wrong, and justify continuing in high, exalted command by protesting that they must follow orders? You bet I am.

I arrived after Operation Hickory, the first of several operations. In the middle of the brawl, a friend of mine, Lieutenant Frank Libutti, was flown in with his platoon. He leaped out of a helicopter into a tangle of Marines and North Viets decked out in tree branches, shooting at one another from fifty feet. A tank was pulling back, while Marines lay wounded on the ground. Libutti pointed his pistol at the panicked tank commander and screamed to get the wounded out of there. The tank swiveled around and the wounded were loaded on board. That week, the Marines lost 142, and 896 were wounded. From an area called Leatherneck Square, some bodies were not recovered for days. Rumors spread that the North Viets had mutilated our dead. The operation was a disaster.

Yet it was repeated, again and again. Common sense demanded that landing from the sea in the enemy's rear and crushing them. A frustrated Marine grunt asked Westmoreland, "General, why can't we go across the DMZ after those bastards?"

He replied, "Politics are such that we can't cross the DMZ."

Westmoreland had wimped out. Politics? At what point does a general speak out if the politics are killing his men? With no maneuver room, each foray resulted in a straight face-to-face clash against an enemy willing to lose hundreds in every fight. One Marine company of 140 grunts staggered out of a clash with 113 killed or wounded.

Why were we doing this? Part of the problem was that the Army and Marine senior officers had fought in Korea a dozen years earlier. Thirty-six thousand Americans died in that confused war that ended in a strained truce. After Korea, a generation officers advanced in rank while lacking a theory of victory that tied battlefield sacrifices to an explicit political end state. As in Korea, the same pattern of see-saw battles of attrition was repeated in Vietnam.

Like waves pounding against the sand, along the DMZ our battalions clashed against the more numerous enemy forces. Chaisson wanted me to write a detailed report on what was happening in these operations. He didn't say so, but I suspected he intended to circulate it as part of building a consensus against the search-and-destroy concept. So, there I was at Con Thien, the same area where I had fought a year earlier. In a tumbling-down bunker, I met with Major Dennis Murphy, a rugged basketball player I knew from my undergraduate days at Georgetown. He gathered his men to relate their fighting experiences.

A few days earlier, Murphy had taken over as the executive officer of Battalion 2/9. The battalion commander had arrived only a day before him. Half of the battalion's six hundred troops were replacements with no combat experience. The battalion was to advance three miles to a hamlet near the Ben Hai River, then come back the next day. The rationale? Brigadier General John Metzger, the Assistant Division Commander of the Third Marine Division, told me, "We wanted to prove to the North Vietnamese that we could enter the DMZ any time we liked."

Expecting a fight, the battalion was reinforced with tanks and other armored vehicles. The grunts complained about a senseless clash on uneven terms before even crossing the line of departure. They muttered, "Another Operation Hickory…keep those tanks away from me…stupidest thing we've ever done."

On the first day, the battalion encountered no resistance and set in for an uneventful night. The next morning, the battalion turned around to head back to Con Thien. Six of the eight tanks and three amtracs were at the front of a long column strung out along the dirt road. A few flankers were sent into the brush and bamboo bordering the road. Low on water and with the temperature rising to a humid ninety-three degrees, the intent was to get out of there as fast as possible.

What they didn't know was that the North Viets had set in mines during the night. Around nine in the morning, the fire team at point lost a Marine in a massive explosion. The dust cloud rising above the undergrowth triggered a barrage of North Vietnamese

82-mm mortar shells. The grunts at the rear of the column froze and went to ground, while those at the front marched on. The lead squad triggered a second mine, then a third. With six Marines dead and a dozen wounded, the front of the column ground forward, now taking rifle fire from both sides of the road. It was well past noon, and the searing sun and battle strain were beating the men down. Out of water, stomach cramps seized several of them.

As the tanks crossed a large clearing, they were struck by several rockets, killing the platoon commander and his radio operator when they stepped out into the open. The shocked platoon refused to cross the clearing. Accompanied by two tanks, the head of the column, including the battalion command group, proceeded toward Con Thien.

The rear of the column hunkered down. The North Viets had them surrounded and drove off the two helicopters trying to land to evacuate the wounded. As the shelling continued, unit cohesion disintegrated. Many troops clustered about the two tanks stranded with them. The men were seized with an obsession to run. They streamed up the road toward the clearing, shucking packs and flak jackets. Wounded were packed onto the two tanks, but both stopped rather than cross the clearing.

The Marines jammed up, with no one providing direction. Half of the battalion were replacements with no combat experience. Few were firing back at the hidden enemy. No offensive forays were launched to clear the flanks or a path forward. Many riflemen turned to aid the wounded instead of returning fire. Others loosed off rounds into vines and bamboo, then slacked off in discouragement at what seemed to be a useless act. Losing fire superiority encouraged the enemy to redouble their efforts, because the chances of being shot had lessened. Those farthest to the rear, not knowing the way ahead was blocked, pushed toward those closer to the kill zone of the open clearing. The A-4 aircraft dropped bombs, but artillery, needed for the close-in fight, was refused by higher headquarters because the jets were in the air.

By late afternoon, hundreds of Marines had clustered in small groups along the sides of the road. The North Viets, clinging to the concealment of the foliage and undergrowth, made no effort to mass and assault. Murphy strode up and down the road, roaring at the grunts to return fire, grabbing small unit leaders and yelling at them to organize their men. As dusk settled in, the enemy fire subsided, stung by repeated air attacks. The A-4 aircraft delivered seventy-three strikes in all. By full dark, the Marines had sorted themselves out into an extended defense. During the night, the North Viets left the battlefield. Twenty-four Marines had died.

In my report to Chaisson, I described the details, concluding that the Marines were definitely and neatly ambushed. A basic mistake was made: unprotected flanks. A lack of planning, to include no quick reaction force, was the other principal mistake. Rarely can a large unit move swiftly or secretly. When a battalion prepared for an operation, telltale signs were there: pre-invasion strikes on the objective, unusual air activity, and so on. This often led to an opening round when the enemy could inflict casualties. After that, if the enemy did not slip away quickly, their forces were mauled. Regardless of the outcome, there were Americans dead in the double figures.

In my conclusion, I wrote, "Battalion operations were a necessary part of the war, but they could be magnified out of proportion to their effectiveness. If large-unit operations had resulted in the destruction or permanent crippling of enemy units, then the massive American military effort in 1966 and '67 would have fundamentally altered the course of the war. A finite time limit on allied casualties could have been predicted. The introduction of fresh troops in a constant stream from North Vietnam would have been an irrational act, had their destruction, unit by unit, been an assured end. In sum, a war of attrition could have succeeded. But that did not happen."

US forces were fighting in an attrition strategy with which they could not win. In writing that conclusion in late 1967, I wasn't opining from a foxhole about grand strategy. Generals Walt and Chaisson had been candid with me. The North Viets kept replacing their losses, while the Marines were forbidden to take the offensive.

That was also the case with our Army units in the southern part of the country. Ordered not to outflank the enemy by forays into Cambodia, Laos, or North Vietnam, and restricted to a narrow front, our troops fought defensive battles that made no strategic sense, and many were poorly executed. Chaisson never told me what he did with my report, and I only briefed General Westmoreland once. His command in Saigon, measuring progress by a kill ratio, persisted in stressing that the North Viets were losing seven to one in the search and destroy operations. The problem was that Hanoi was willing to lose thirty to one and keep on fighting.

"Vietnam is a return to medieval war," Walt had written, "pitting man against man on a battleground where only the courageous could win." Much as I admired the general as a warrior, courage wasn't enough. America needed a sound strategy.

CHAPTER 3

Battle in Vietnam:
Interim Success

In late 1967, I went to work for The RAND Corporation, a think tank. RAND's brain trust kibitzed with the Secretaries of Defense and with the White House. My job was to contribute to an understanding of the counterinsurgency program. In early December, as part of a multi-month trip around Vietnam, I again visited the village of Binh Nghia.

The fifteen Marines in the CAP had arrived in the village in June of 1966. In Binh Nghia, the Marines had no way of distinguishing a guerrilla from a civilian. They did, however, dominate in the night fights. This gave the PFs under Suong the confidence to move against those suspected of being VC agents. The villagers didn't raise their hoes and rakes to drive out the insurgents. But by whispers, they pointed out suspects. Suong's men cleared the village; the Marines provided the firepower and the example. The villagers accepted the Marines because they were willing to fight. They brought no money or construction projects. All they left behind was one concrete well and their example of courage. Nine had paid with their lives.

By October 1967, the firefights had died out. After 385 days, the Marines' job seemed finished, and the command pulled them out. It was then up to Suong to hold Binh Nghia. He insisted to me that the fight wasn't over. His nemesis—the P-31st Viet Cong company that had killed Joe Sullivan, Phil Brannon, and the others—was still out there, biding its time. Much to his dissatisfaction, I told him I could do nothing.

After visiting Suong in early December of 1967, I took a ferry down the Song Tra Bong to catch up with Captain Philip Volentine, the district advisor. He wanted a CAP in every one of the twenty-six villages in the district. Phil was on edge, convinced an attack was coming. He asked me to stay the night. But the general commanding a nearby Army division sent a colonel to invite me to dinner. I accepted because the general controlled my access. Phil warned us the P-31st was gathering to strike. It wasn't yet twilight, but no people were on the dirt street. The shops were closed. Nonsense, the colonel said; his division, called the American, had killed five hundred NVA.

"Colonel," Volentine replied, "that's your war, not mine."

Major General Samuel Koster commanded the American Division. At dinner, he firmly but politely rejected my suggestion that his soldiers adapt the CAP concept. He had agreed to allow eight Marine CAPs to remain after his division had arrived; however, he would not expand the program. He said that the fundamental premise of the CAP was wrong. The mission of his soldiers was to search and destroy the Viet Cong and the NVA. Village security was a local matter to be handled by the PFs. Dinner was interrupted by an aide who said the district post had just been blown up and Volentine was dead. I flew in with a company of soldiers. Volentine's concrete bunker building lay crushed. Half of the town's shanties, plywood mixed with thatch, were burned to ash.

I moved on to a nearby CAP, where the grunts were gossiping about the resignation of Secretary of Defense Robert McNamara. After he told Johnson the war could not be won, the president moved him out of office. On the streets, college protesters were chanting, "Ho ho, Ho Chi Minh is gonna win." In his kitchen, McNamara had cried in sympathy with a student refusing to serve. What tears were shed for Brannon, Volentine, or the nameless replacement killed in the palm grove a few hours after arriving? McNamara had broken faith with the troops he sent into battle.

Then, during the Tet holiday of early February 1968, the leaders in Hanoi ordered a massive countrywide assault by about eighty-five thousand Viet Cong and North Vietnamese soldiers. They foolishly believed the urban populations would rise in their favor. Instead, fully half of the attackers were killed. The mainstream press, however, depicted Tet as a victory for the enemy. Tet solidified political opposition to the war in the States.

* * *

At about the same time, RAND hired Charlie Benoit, an all-American lacrosse player at Yale whose fluency in Vietnamese was astonishing. Despite his massive size, his empathetic manner put Vietnamese people at ease. We teamed up, and for three years, we shuttled between RAND's office in Santa Monica and Vietnam, visiting twenty-six of the forty-four provinces.

Year after year, we reported from the countryside. On one visit back to Binh Nghia, we set in a night ambush with Suong's PFs along the river. Bored after an hour, Charlie went into a hooch to talk with an old fisherman. His delighted host proceeded to recount his family history, starting in the sixteenth century. Charlie was deep asleep when those of us outside tangled with some Viet Cong. As the red and green tracers zipped past each other, I heard a deep thumping. In the pitch dark, Charlie was hurling his bulk at a bamboo wall until he burst through.

Another time, as I followed Charlie through a hamlet, the kids ran away and the adults slammed their doors shut. I was carrying a loose haversack with my Swedish K submachine gun and several clips inside. It jingled as I walked. In Vietnam, rural dentists carry a pouch containing teeth they have pulled to prove their skill. Charlie warned the people that I was a disgraced American dentist. My haversack, Charlie told the villagers, was bulging because it was filled with broken teeth. Stay away from the American dentist.

In the summer of 1968, Charlie and I returned to the hardscrabble district of Dai Loc, adjacent to the mountains forty miles southwest of the city of Da Nang. When I passed through there on my way to see Phil Volentine in 1967, the district headquarters had been defended by a full battalion. The NVA had burned the outlying hamlets because they seemed too friendly toward the Americans. Eight months later, the NVA had been pushed deeper into the jungle and five refugee camps had been built, enclosed in barbed wire and consisting of neat rows of plywood huts with tin roofs. A CAP was assigned to each camp. The total American presence had dropped from about one thousand to one hundred.

We arrived amid commotion. The previous day, Marines from a CAP had caught eighteen refugees depositing sacks of rice at a river crossing used by NVA scouts. Accusing them of selling rice, the Marines brought them to the district chief. The district chief released seventeen refugees. He detained the man who had organized the sale, who promptly escaped two hours later. When the CAP Marines accused the chief as being a traitor, the province governor had intervened. Then Charlie and I arrived. Eyeing us nervously, he made a show of firing the district chief. The chief responded that the released man had agreed to act as a double agent. The governor then abruptly left, declaring the matter closed.

Charlie walked outside to chat with the refugees, who told their side of the story. They indignantly insisted they hadn't done anything wrong. The government gave them rice each month. On their own, they were growing acres of corn that they ate, while selling the rice. The man who "escaped" brokered the price. They needed money and had been burned out once already. If they didn't sell the rice, the NVA would burn them out as soon as the Americans left.

The incident summarized the countryside. The loyalties and effectiveness of government officials were a kaleidoscope, shifting amid factional bickering and local patronage. Could any US advisor on a six-month tour unravel the fictions or persuade officials to refuse bribes for their extended family? After four years of traveling everywhere and talking with thousands of villagers, Charlie had concluded that the government lacked the power to impose basic standards of performance. With no central system for promotion based on merit, every district was sui generis. Charlie cautioned that when the CAP Marines left, the refugees in Dai Loc would resume doing business with the North Vietnamese. The people were the prize, not the means of winning the war.

Back at RAND in Santa Monica, we weren't rated as among the top rank of Vietnam analysts. The top spot went to Daniel Ellsberg, an intellectual courtesan who betrayed the trust reposed in him. In my opinion, Charlie deserved to lead the RAND effort in Vietnam. He was enrolled in the PhD program at Harvard, fluent in Vietnamese, respected by everyone, fearless, and deeply conversant with the Byzantine politics, causing him to conclude the government was too fragmented to unite its people.

In Santa Monica, I listened to RAND's brilliant men, such as Albert Wohlstetter, Herman Kahn, and Nathan Leites, expound theories in intellectual jousting matches. The emphasis was upon logical thinking, far removed from the violence and blood Charlie and I saw in the field. Harvard professors Thomas Schelling and Henry Kissinger frequently visited, analyzing how North Vietnam's leaders might be persuaded to negotiate. Perhaps had *The Gulag Archipelago* been printed earlier, these intelligent men would have understood the ruthless implacability of the Stalinist politburo in Hanoi.

Charlie Benoit, warrior/diplomat.

* * *

In the fall of 1968, Charlie and I were in treacherous Dien Ban district, twenty miles south of Da Nang. We were tracking rumors of arms sales by South Vietnamese soldiers. The district advisors, after warning it was crazy to go into the market, loaned me a PRC-25 radio to call if in trouble. Walking among marketplace shoppers haggling over the price of chickens, puppies, duck eggs, rice, we could felt resentment and incredulity at our presence. Charlie couldn't coax anyone to chat.

Then a dozen shabbily dressed Vietnamese, all heavily armed, approached us. Charlie reached into the haversack for our Swedish K, while I picked up the handset of the PRC radio. A stocky figure tapped the barrel of his carbine against his leg, shook his head, and took off his bush hat. With his tortoiseshell eyeglasses and unassuming manner, he looked like a mild-mannered American high school teacher.

"No friendlies out here," he said. "Not the right place for you to be. We'll escort you back."

That's how I met Rudy Enders, the covert CIA warrior who became director of Special Operations Group. The mean-looking Viets with him were PRUs, or Provincial Reconnaissance Units. PRUs were testy and volatile, knowing they operated under a VC death sentence. Their target had fled when we popped in and wandered around. Rudy warmed to the two of us, a Marine grunt and huge athlete whose Vietnamese was pitch perfect. He put out the word in CIA circles to help Charlie and me. On our travels over the next three years, we received quiet assistance and inside advice from the CIA rep in every district we visited.

In 1962, Rudy had put ashore in Cuba a team of exiles that discovered the Soviet nuclear missiles, provoking the Cuban Missile Crisis. President John F. Kennedy dispatched a U-2 spy plane to photograph the missiles in order not to blow Rudy's team's cover. Unfortunately, Castro's forces did uncover and execute the team.

Rudy's escapades were folklore inside the CIA. In Tet of 1968, he rescued his Vietnamese wife Ngoc by driving a motorcycle under fire in Hue City, when Marines were fighting street by street against several thousand North Vietnamese. In 1975, as South Vietnam was falling, he flew daily in a small plane to call in hundreds of air strikes upon the advancing North Vietnamese. In 1979, he flew a rickety transport aircraft to the frontlines in Angola to rescue British mercenaries on the CIA's payroll. In 1982, he flew a helicopter from a clandestine ship onto a beach in hostile Nicaragua and swam out into the surf to rescue two stranded third-country operatives.

When we arrived back at Dien Ban district headquarters, a squad of angry CAP Marines were waiting. They took us to a crumbling hamlet called Hoa Phon. Shouting and screeching, the village elders tugged us over to a well in the hamlet square. They explained to Charlie that they couldn't drink the water because bodies were rotting down there. The furious Marines said South Korean troops, having taken fire on a nearby road, had retaliated by shooting villagers and hurling their bodies down the well.

We reported this to Major General Ray Tompkins. He said no Marine was a direct eyewitness. But he strongly suggested we report it to Washington. A month later, Deputy Secretary of State Elliot Richardson called us in. He listened intently and remonstrated with the South Korean ambassador. When *The Washington Post* picked up our story, Secretary of Defense Melvin Laird explained that the Koreans operated under their own chain of command. Too many in the press, though, persisted in praising the Koreans for a toughness that was actually cruelty.

We had our own breakdowns in basic humanity. More than a hundred soldiers in the American Division committed the massacre at My Lai in March 1968, gunning down more than a hundred women and children. It took years, but that shameful act was eventually exposed. Maj Gen Koster, with whom I had dinner as Phil Volentine was dying, retired in disgrace. What happened there was not who we are as a people. It was a moral stain that should be remembered. The root causes were wretched leadership and callous officers furious after taking continuous casualties from mines and snipers.

Charlie and I first heard about it from bewildered CAP Marines. We visited the forlorn hamlet of My Lai, only four miles from Binh Nghia. "That couldn't happen in Binh Nghia," Charlie said to me. "The Marines couldn't destroy their own village. What would they say? Sorry, we forgot we live here?"

* * *

When we returned again to Binh Nghia in October 1968, Suong asked us to cross the Tra Bong river with his platoon into the mine-infested Phu Longs, lair of the P-31st VC company. He wanted us along to call in fire, while the PFs rustled cows from their Viet Cong neighbors. When I refused to risk my legs for the sake of some scrawny cows, Charlie said I had become uncharacteristically calculating about running risks. Conversely, I suspected Charlie was willing to cross over, hoping to chat with the enemy about their point of view. He had met twice with a North Viet colonel at some rendezvous spot. I thought his curiosity about other points of view would get him snatched.

We wished Suong luck and hitched a ride downriver to the CAP at Binh Thuy village, where news was buzzing about the death of a feared guerrilla. Quiet Corporal Gene Foster told us he had been out on a night patrol when he had the feeling he was being stalked. He backed into the dark cover of a hooch, safety off, and stood motionless. Hearing a slight rustle, he ripped through a whole magazine. His bullets tore up a Viet Cong company commander notorious for killing PFs in their beds. As we talked, villagers passing by smiled and waved at him. Foster shrugged off the congratulations. He was prouder of providing food to a poor family. A week after our visit, an assassin killed him.

That's how it went. We had compassionate, tough grunts like Foster. But the North Viets were determined to seize the south, regardless of how many of their soldiers died.

From 1967 through 1969, Charlie and I visited sixty districts in fifteen of Vietnam's eighteen provinces to assess rural security. Thanks to his amiable manner and astonishing fluency, wherever we went, the residents usually warned us if we were in danger. On one occasion, we hired a taxi instead of walking a few miles. Without hesitation, the driver took us back to the district market and demanded to be paid. Tigers were up the road, he explained, waiting to eat us. When Charlie asked if the tigers walked on two legs, the driver nodded.

*　*　*

There were also real tigers. When I was on patrol with Lieutenant Tony Monroe's platoon one night, we were walking single file through chest-high grass, with a sharp wind in our faces. To our front, a water buffalo in a fenced-in pen was bellowing and pawing the ground. As we skirted around, a deep growl from the grass froze us. Then the grass whipped back and forth as the big cat raced back and forth parallel to our file, looking for an opening to escape. Corporal Washington loosed a burst from his M-14. The cat screeched, leaped straight into the air, and was gone. No one hurt.

Recon Marines in the jungles around the Rockpile near Laos were not as fortunate. In 1968, the huge cat in the picture below pounced on a Marine on sentry duty deep in the bush. The tiger dragged his prey into a nearby shell hole. The other five Marines slipped into the hole, killed the four-hundred-pound cat, and rescued their comrade.

In typical bureaucratic fashion, the injured Marine was initially denied a Purple Heart because the tiger wasn't a human enemy. It took a general's order to overturn that absurdity.

* * *

Charlie and I encountered our own unfriendly cats. One time, we hopped a bus to an outlying "contested" village, without bringing a military radio. Charlie was carrying only a pistol and in my pack, I had the Swedish K submachine gun, with barrel disconnected. We sauntered into a bar, a cement hovel with swinging doors copied from Hollywood Westerns. When we sat down, the two dozen armed patrons stopped talking. A disbelieving, bilious badass knocked over his beer and yelled in Vietnamese, "What the hell are round-eyed invaders doing in here?" Great. We had no idea who the armed drunks were, but their astonishment and hatred were evident. I watched one tapping his carbine. But before they could gather their wits, Charlie talked our way out the swinging doors. We dodged through the foliage for a kilometer before hitching a ride in a melon truck back to district headquarters.

* * *

By 1970, the security situation in the countryside had definitely improved. Bombed and pursued continuously, the NVA had pulled back deeper into the mountains and jungles. The Viet Cong guerrilla apparatus was so heavily damaged in the 1968 Tet Offensive that it never regained its dominance. Most of our wanderings over the years had been in those contested areas where the NVA could reinforce the guerrillas. Charlie wanted to assess conditions where there were no northerners. We contacted Enders, who put us in touch with CIA operatives and SEALs in the Mekong Delta two hundred miles south of Saigon. We flew down to the Gia Rai district in Bac Lieu Province. The SEALs took us on a few raids. They were competent fighters, but disinterested in the politics underlying the pacification program.

Charlie split off to spend time with Major Quyet, the district chief. Quyet was capable, candid, and disillusioned. The people did warn him when the Viet Cong gathered a few times a year for military assaults. Of course, the people knew who among them belonged to the guerrilla infrastructure—the leader, the tax collector, the enforcers, and so on. No one pointed them out. If a VC was captured, the police decided what evidence was admissible and what court arraignment was suitable. Usually, small sums of money changed hands along the way. What difference would it make if small-time operators went free?

"Quyet stated categorically," Charlie wrote in our report, "that without the US, within twenty-four hours the situation would deteriorate completely." Even where the North Vietnamese did not have a presence, the government was not functioning effectively, allowing the Viet Cong to bide its time.

* * *

We went back a few times each year to Binh Nghia, our lodestone. Binh Nghia was one of a dozen villages scattered among salt-encrusted paddies on the Batangan peninsula, seventy miles south of Danang. To avoid presenting a target, by 1970, the North Vietnamese had dispersed into groups of six to ten soldiers scattered on the jungle hillsides ten miles west of the peninsula. They joined with local guerrillas about once a month to conduct an assault, then spread out again.

The American Division was supposed to prevent these raids. But the American made no effort to link together the scattered CAPs or to tap into the village rumor networks. Instead, the soldiers slept inside large, fixed bases from which they launched patrols and raids via helicopters. In the sad book entitled *Our War*, David Taylor described the circumstances around the death of each of the sixty-four soldiers killed in his battalion. On page after page, he described sweeps and mines and snipers and ambushes, together with the names and ages of the soldiers killed day after day. Taylor, on his second tour, wrote, "a patrol came upon a bunker and was hit with small arms fire.… There was no stomach from the soldiers for fire and maneuver. Three years earlier an assault would have been routinely made when winning a war was still possible."

Every grunt had a sense for the odds. By 1970, the grunts in the American were understandably cautious as US forces withdrew. Why be the last soldier to die?

Whenever we returned to Binh Nghia, the elders lobbied for Marines to come back. At its peak, the CAP program encompassed eight hundred hamlets, protecting 500,000 villagers.[1] Not one CAP village was ever retaken by the Viet Cong or NVA. But there never was a plan to tie the CAPs together like a honeycomb. General Westmoreland believed the CAPs were too manpower-intensive and too slow in pacifying. No top-level meeting was ever convened to resolve the Army-Marine dispute. To quote from the official Marine history, "The problem was a lack of a war-fighting [overall] strategy. There was no yardstick for measuring the amount of resources dedicated to Mission X vs. Mission Y."[2]

Throughout our travels even in 1970, Charlie and I heard one consistent message from the Viet Cong: "The Americans are going home, and then we'll be back." Despite much less fighting, the fear of death hung over the hamlets. Charlie was convinced the South's senior leaders were too divided among themselves, lacking the cohesion and national message to unify the rural population.

* * *

I wrote a book, *The Village*, chronicling what happened over those 385 days when the Marines had lived and died among the villagers in Binh Nghia.

In 2002, twenty-seven years after South Vietnam fell, Charlie and I went back to Binh Nghia. The North Vietnamese had changed the name of the village because Americans had lived there. That didn't impress the villagers, who turned out in large numbers to greet us warmly.

The author back in Binh Nghia, 2002.

We learned the fates of those we had known long ago. Trao, the village chief, had drowned while fishing. Ho Chi, the school teacher, had been killed trying to escape the country in 1975. Suong had died when he opened a gate rigged with a grenade. For eight years, he had patrolled within the same dozen kilometers. He knew by name at least five hundred of the villagers. Although he was valiant and shrewd, no one can survive indefinitely as a grunt. Sooner or later, the bell tolls.

A brilliant quantitative analyst at RAND, Carl Morris, and I used a primitive computer to enter 1,154 sitreps (situation reports) filed by battalions over six months. In 75 percent of the firefights, the Marines reported no friendly or known enemy fatalities. In 20 percent of the fights, one or more enemies were killed, with no friendly fatalities. In 5 percent of the fights, one or more Marines died.

What does that tell you about close combat? Most of the time, you engage the enemy and have no idea if you did any damage. Due to better training, in one out of five fights, you do kill an enemy, and in one out of twenty fights, you lose a brother. In World War II, bomber crews were rotated back to the States after completing a set number of missions. Why? Because not returning was inevitable if the pilot flew throughout the war. Serving in the infantry in Vietnam was the same way. A year of patrolling took a staggering toll. Most commanders tried to send the frontline grunts, after six or eight months, to safer jobs in the rear.

There was no rear for Suong. And in 1975, there was no rear for all South Vietnamese soldiers. Many were imprisoned for years. Their families were herded into ghettos and their children mocked as *con nguy*—child of a puppet. When we returned in 2002, the mama sans pored over pictures of the CAP Marines who had lived in their village, recalling names. Corporal Phil Brannon was called "Phbill." The village chief met with us, explaining he was one of the many urchins wandering about the fort back then. He said the village had doubled in size to ten thousand. He needed more land and better rice seed. Charlie responded that he should ask the government.

"Those northerners don't care about us," he said. "You lived with us. They didn't."

CHAPTER 4

Vietnam Policy: Why We Lost

From 1965 through 1975, I both participated in the fighting and, during assignments in Washington, had the opportunity to observe firsthand how our policymakers dealt with the war. While working for RAND, I briefed top military and civilian officials, including General William Westmoreland. When the US combat involvement wound down in 1970, I left RAND to join the quantitative analysts, cynically nicknamed "the whiz kids," in the Pentagon's Office of Systems Analysis. I got along well with the crusty Chairman of the Joint Chiefs of Staff, Admiral Tom Moorer, and Secretary of Defense Melvin Laird, who sent me to Cambodia to assess the local forces there. In my next job in 1973 as Director of Research at the Naval War College in Newport, RI, I listened to dozens of colonels reflect on their command experiences in Vietnam. In 1975, I served as Special Assistant to Secretary of Defense Jim Schlesinger as South Vietnam entered its death throes.

What did I take away from listening to those at the top? As will be explained in this chapter, I concluded that the primary reason for losing was that our policymakers believed we were too rich and too powerful to lose. So, we didn't have to undertake a harsh, unyielding military course. We didn't have to bomb the dikes and divert North Vietnamese soldiers into rice pickers. We didn't have to blockade the harbors and cut off the arms supplies from Russia and China. We didn't have to blast and fortify a barrier across Laos. By signaling that we were stronger, we could persuade the hard, dedicated leaders of North Vietnam to desist from attacking the south. Believing that because we were stronger we would naturally prevail was the basic misconception underlying all the other mistakes.

The war can be divided into two timeframes: 1965 to 1968, and 1969 to 1975.

1965–1968: President Lyndon B. Johnson's War

From 1965 until leaving office in January of 1969, President Lyndon B. Johnson refused to believe that the Lao Dong Party in North Vietnam was implacable in its determination to seize the South. Johnson was the consummate deal-maker. In his view, all he had to do was find the right combination of bluff, bribe, and violence to end the war.

In July 1965, the Joint Chiefs of Staff opined that there was "no reason we cannot win if such is our will—and if that will is manifested in strategy and tactical operations."[1] They estimated deploying 700,000 to a million US troops for seven years, plus heavy bombing of the North, cutting off all aid coming from China and the Soviet Union, and amphibious landings in the rear of the NVA. When they collectively presented their strategy to Johnson, he flew into a rage and cursed them as "assholes trying to get him to start World War III [against China]."[2] A bully at heart, Johnson threw them out of the Oval Office, severing the relationship with his military advisors. Not one of the humiliated generals resigned or went public about LBJ's dismissal of their combined military judgment. Johnson made Vietnam *his* war, to be conducted *his* way, ever fearful of China.

Mao Tse-tung did believe in global revolution and fulsomely supported the North Vietnamese politburo. Within two years, 170,000

Chinese troops would be providing air defense gun crews and logistic support in North Vietnam. But because his army had been chewed up by the Americans in the Korean War, he set a firm line: Chinese troops could operate only north of the 21st Parallel, 300 miles from South Vietnam.[3] Johnson intuitively concluded the opposite and that drove his vacillating approach to the war. There is no evidence that the CIA tried to disabuse him of his incorrect assumption.

Having antagonized the Joint Chiefs of Staff, Johnson asked former President Dwight Eisenhower for his advice. Eisenhower urged him not to vacillate or adopt gradualism, thereby allowing the enemy time to adjust. "Eisenhower was convinced that Johnson," wrote historian Stephen Ambrose, "showed a lack of the firm commitment needed to achieve victory in Vietnam. He felt Johnson ignored his advice to either go all-in with a clear strategy or disengage, believing anything less betrayed a weakness of resolve."[4] Instead, Johnson took heed of President Harry Truman's political fate. Caught by surprise when North Korea, with Stalin's approval, invaded South Korea in June 1950, Truman rushed in troops. He avoided asking Congress for a declaration of war, concerned the Republicans would blame him for being unprepared for the invasion. He claimed the fighting was only "a police action." By late fall, US forces were advancing north to control the entire Korean peninsula. Chairman Mao Tse-tung responded by sending in hundreds of thousands of Chinese soldiers to keep American forces from reaching his doorstep. The war then dragged on for two years, making Truman so unpopular that he did not run for re-election.

In 1965, Lyndon Johnson concluded that he must not take any action that might cause China to enter the war, however remote that chance. He persuaded Congress not to declare war, but instead to authorize him employ force as he deemed fit. This gave him total flexibility in choosing the amount of force and the end goal. Determined not to upset China, he treated North Vietnam as a sanctuary, forbidding any blockade of its ports or ground incursions. This permitted the Soviet Union and China to provide North Vietnam, which lacked an industrial base, with tens of thousands of advisors, artillery tubes, tanks, trucks, and air defense missiles. In conversations he secretly taped with senators, Johnson said he saw "no way to win the war militarily."[5] In his judgment, the war was a matter to be settled by bargaining. He alternately launched and suspended seven bombing campaigns over North Vietnam, proffering bombing pauses to induce negotiations. He also offered to pay for massive dams to improve North Vietnam's electric power grid. He never grasped the Stalinist iron will of the Lao Dong Party, which was willing to sacrifice millions of lives.

With the Joint Chiefs of Staff stripped of influence, the ground war became the purview of Westmoreland, the commander in Vietnam from 1964 to mid-1968. Early on, Westmoreland had proposed deploying three US divisions (about 120,000 soldiers) across Laos, a tribal country controlled by North Vietnam. The defensive line across Korea today is 150 miles long. From Vietnam across Laos to Thailand is 120 miles. In retrospect, it was the only feasible solution. In Washington in 1965, however, it was rejected out of hand as too drastic.

Westmoreland then had to decide between trying to regain control of the rural population or destroying the NVA forces flowing into the South. He chose the latter, believing he would win by attrition. He assumed that when enough North Vietnamese soldiers were killed, the Lao Dong Party would desist. He left it to the South Vietnamese forces to defeat the Viet Cong guerrillas and control the rural population. He did grudgingly allow the Marines at the northern top of the country to pursue counterinsurgency, as well engage the NVA in a grim slugfest.

The Marines' measure of success was knitting together village militias to destroy the guerrilla government apparatus in the countryside. South Vietnamese and US Marine battalions would repulse external assault by North Vietnamese divisions. The Marines, however, did not systematically tie in all the villages. More devastating, between 1966 and 1968, hundreds of thousands of North

Viet soldiers poured in. Gradually, the guerrillas were beaten down, but the North Viets kept coming on in large numbers, despite being pounded.

Westmoreland's measure of success was maintaining a kill ratio of about ten North Vietnamese to one American soldier. In Korea, killing until the enemy agreed to a ceasefire in 1953 had succeeded. Eisenhower's threat to use nuclear weapons also played a role, as did the strong defensive line across the peninsula. Lacking any such line across Laos upon which to embed a defense, Westmoreland believed there was a demographic crossover point at which the North would lose more young men than they could replace. The CIA strongly disagreed. North Vietnam was willing to lose millions; the American public wasn't willing to lose one hundred thousand in return. The CIA and Westmoreland's command never resolved their basic disagreement.

Secretary of Defense Robert McNamara, as feckless as Johnson, also wanted only to demonstrate to North Vietnam that the odds were against their winning. In 1967, he told Johnson the war could not be won. Johnson fired him. Years later, at Schlesinger's home, McNamara severely lectured me for not understanding war's complexities. Johnson replaced him with Clark Clifford, who said, "We're not out to win the war. We're out to win the peace." That sappy sentiment reflected a person already defeated. Wars are fought to impose your will upon the enemy. If you don't intend to win, don't accept the position of Secretary of Defense.

From 1965 through 1968, Johnson fought a halfhearted war. Historians have since blotted out his indecisiveness. Our grunts did not have that choice; thirty thousand died under his watch. As Justice Oliver Wendell Holmes wrote, "To fight out a war, you must believe something and want something with all your might."[6] Johnson never grasped that. In his view, America was stronger. Once the enemy understood that, a reasonable settlement would be reached. He wasn't a wartime president; he initiated a war he never intended to win. He did not grasp his role as president and commander in chief: He did not keep faith with those who placed their faith in him.

1969–1973: President Richard Nixon's War

In late 1969, Richard Nixon took office, convinced that the American political mood required pulling US troops out without the world concluding that we had quit. He and his key aide, Henry Kissinger, believed American credibility required an "honorable" exit. After visiting several battlefields in 1966, Kissinger had advocated adopting the Marine counterinsurgency strategy and firing Westmoreland. Three years later, he agreed with Nixon that "the US could no longer achieve its objectives within a [reasonable time] period and with force levels politically acceptable to the American people."[7]

Nixon ordered the steady drawdown of US troops. General Creighton Abrams, who replaced Westmoreland, began turning the war over to the South Vietnamese. In the rural countryside, counterinsurgency was catching hold, and the NVA was being driven deeper into the jungles. By 1970, daytime traffic was moving unmolested throughout most of the populated areas.

Two years later, only seventy thousand US troops, mostly logistic units, remained in the country. The South Vietnamese government seemed to be more cohesive. To regain the initiative, the North Vietnamese mounted a massive armored assault in 1972. A quarter of a million NVA soldiers, supported by a thousand tanks, launched a tri-headed offensive in the northern and central sectors of South Vietnam, together with a sustained push farther south.

Nixon responded by ordering heavy bombing across the North, cutting supplies to the frontline troops by 70 percent. Downtown Hanoi shook under successive B-52 raids, and the port of Hanoi was blockaded, cutting off military equipment and munitions from Russia and China. In the South, American advisors orchestrated forty thousand air strikes. The North was pushed back with casualties approaching a hundred thousand. The victory showed that the South could persevere, provided US supplies and airpower could be called upon. The North Vietnamese political leaders were further shaken by the B-52 onslaught against Hanoi in December of 1972. Unfortunately, Nixon intended only to force negotiations. Documents later revealed the Lao Dong leadership was on the verge of splintering and desisting.

In January 1973, Kissinger signed a peace treaty removing all US combat troops, while North Vietnamese divisions remained in the South, ready to pounce. The kicker was that Nixon had secretly promised to give the South the same number of arms that the Soviets and Chinese were providing to the North. As important, he pledged massive air strikes if the North launched another offensive.

In June 1973, however, Nixon was ensnared and paralyzed by his cover-up of a bungled burglary at the Watergate condominiums. The Democrats, controlling both branches of Congress, had turned vehemently against the war. Congress passed legislation forbidding US air strikes anywhere in Southeast Asia and slashed aid to South Vietnam. Nixon resigned in disgrace, replaced by Republican Congressman Gerald Ford.

In 1974, Secretary of Defense Jim Schlesinger asked me to leave the Naval War College and serve as his special assistant. He had a soft spot for combat grunts. His favorite officers were General Louis Wilson, the Medal of Honor Marine Commandant, and Abrams, recently returned from Vietnam. It was a sour time to be in the Pentagon. Secretary of State Kissinger had pivoted to assuring the Soviet Union that America's accommodative goal was détente. President Ford followed along, indifferent to the war's outcome. Schlesinger was the only senior official actively trying to garner aid for South Vietnam. He invited to breakfast every senator and congressman. He showed the Soviet and Chinese weaponry flowing into the North versus the dwindling munitions in the South. Give them the ammo to fight, he asked. The congressional reply was an indignant no. Without military aid or air support, South Vietnam was doomed to fall after, as Kissinger infelicitously expressed it, "a decent interval."[8] Saigon fell in April of 1975.

Schlesinger immediately reached out to our troops. "Your record of duty performed under difficult conditions is unmatched," he wrote. "You are entitled to the nation's respect, admiration, and gratitude."[9]

Secretary of Defense James Schlesinger and author, 1975.

Fifty-six thousand Americans died in Vietnam. Seventy percent of those killed were volunteers. Ninety-one percent of all Vietnam veterans and 90 percent of those who saw heavy combat are proud to have served their country.[10] They were treated shabbily by the press and by the college protesters of their own age.

The post-war narrative in the American press has stressed that the fall of South Vietnam was inevitable. Nonsense. History is a record of human decisions; it is not pre-determined. Defeat was no more inevitable in South Vietnam than was our long-term victory in South Korea. By withdrawing its logistic support and the threat of resuming a bombing campaign, America chose to lose South Vietnam.

After the American forces left in 1972, the Viet Cong did not reemerge as the dominant force in the countryside. In our travels, Charlie Benoit had concluded that the central government in Saigon was too fractured to solidify the gains in the countryside over the long term (say, ten or more years). However, the end came much more quickly in 1975, due to a massive conventional assault from the North, and not due to a simmering insurgency.

"Vietnam succumbed," Schlesinger wrote, "to powerful external forces."[11] Russia and China consistently aided the Stalinist party of North Vietnam that sacrificed a million soldiers to achieve its goal. War is determined by capability and will. North Vietnam defeated America because its will was much stronger, even while its capability was inferior. Historians absolved their favored Lyndon Johnson and gave a pass to Gerald Ford as being of limited acumen. They concentrated their fire on Nixon as tricky and devious. That is reducing history to an evaluation of personalities.

In response to student protests, the draft was abolished; only volunteers need fight in the future. Vietnam set a terrible precedent for indecisiveness and lack of moral conviction in prosecuting a war. It ripped apart the fabric of shared patriotism and trust in our national leaders. A persisting cultural effect was a negative view of our country held and taught by college professors. This infected generations of Americans. That is the enduring, scorching legacy of our defeat in Vietnam.

After the fall of Saigon in 1975, American foreign policy manifested serious dyspepsia. In supplicant fashion, we courted détente—"Can't we all just get along?"—with a supposedly stronger Soviet Union, and we permitted an Islamist theocratic rabble to seize our embassy officials in Iran. Only gradually did we recover. In 1981, President Ronald Reagan took office, rebuilt our military, challenged the Soviet Union and abetted in its demise.

CHAPTER 5

Battle in Iraq

I n Iraq a quarter of a century later, I saw that same White House overconfidence in our military capabilities and the same lack of consistent will on the part of our policymakers. On September 11, 2001, Islamist terrorists crashed two aircraft into the Twin Towers in New York City, killing three thousand civilians. Al Qaeda had plotted the attack from Afghanistan. Within a few months, CIA and Army Special Forces teams were on the ground supporting Afghan warlords by calling in massive air strikes. The Al Qaeda and Taliban main forces quickly disintegrated, and the survivors fled into Pakistan. By 2003, Afghanistan seemed stable, requiring relatively few US forces.

President George W. Bush then decided to remove Saddam Hussein, who ruled Iraq, because the CIA and many NATO intelligence agencies believed he was developing weapons of mass destruction (WMD). The danger was that he might give WMD to Islamists to attack America. Accordingly, in early 2003, the Congress and the UN approved the invasion of Iraq. (Only later was the WMD assumption shown to be false.) An allied force (mostly American) of 200,000 troops had assembled in Kuwait.

I decided to cover the invasion as a writer. My friend, Ray Smith, joined me as coauthor. A retired two-star general, Ray was perhaps the most decorated Marine from Vietnam. He was part of the small force that slugged it out against ten thousand North Vietnamese holding Hue in 1968. He entered the city as a lieutenant in a company of 144 grunts; he left a month later in charge of a company of seventeen. In 1972, for a full day he carried on his shoulders a wounded Vietnamese officer through the jungle to safety, pursued by hundreds of North Vietnamese soldiers. He was called "E-Tool" for having killed two North Viets with an entrenching tool. His tactical competence and valor were legendary. Like Rudy Enders in the CIA, Ray Smith belongs in the pantheon of American warriors.

We arrived in Kuwait in February 2003, without any book contract or press credentials. Major General Jim Mattis, commanding the forty-thousand-man 1st Marine Division, welcomed us as fellow Marines. However, a general above him in the chain of command, concerned about what we might write, insisted we go back to the States. Ray angrily confronted him and he backed down. We returned to the division, where Mattis told us to move where we pleased among his units once the attack began. But, he added, don't become a news story by being killed.

In March, the invasion unfolded with overpowering force. Saddam's headquarters was in Baghdad, four hundred miles across swampy ground north of Kuwait. Seven thousand Marine vehicles advanced on a few long columns, restricted by swampy ground on either side. Twenty miles to the west, two US Army divisions were likewise pushing forward. Mattis's intent was to feint, push around, and fight through several Iraqi divisions to reach Baghdad before Saddam could organize a defense.

On the second day, a regimental commander, Colonel Steve Hummer, offered Ray and me a captured yellow Nissan SUV and a military radio. We no longer had to hitch rides. For the eighteen days of the invasion, we cut from unit to unit, staying with the action. I took notes and pictures, while Ray tracked our routes and drove with wild dirt bike skill.

On the third day, we parked by a soccer field where a dozen Iraqi soldiers were dug in on the far side. Beyond the field, I saw four or five men darting around, dressed in black, Ninja-like out-fits, complete with black masks over their faces. Rocket-propelled grenades sailed over us, exploding harmlessly on telephone wires. The Marines set up two machine guns, forcing the Iraqis to keep their heads down while a platoon (of about forty grunts) dashed for-ward by bounds. The Iraqis responded with a fusillade of wild shots before they were killed. No Marine was scratched.

We trotted forward behind the platoon. A corpsman was work-ing on the fatally punctured stomach of a fat, middle-aged Iraqi major in a starched green uniform and clean white underwear. A shot of morphine had dulled his pain. His blood had turned the dirt into mud, and his lips were bluish. He looked bewildered that his life was draining away. More in exasperation than anger, the platoon sergeant bent over the dying man.

"What were you doing, man?" he said. "You don't belong out here."

On the fourth day, we reached a four-lane bridge leading into the scruffy city of Nasiriyah. At this juncture, one Marine regiment in two thousand vehicles was supposed to pass through the lines of another, an operational hazard waiting to happen. When the lead unit was hit inside the city, thousands of vehicles jammed up at the bridge into the city.

Under Mattis were three colonels, each commanding a regimental combat team (RCT) of nine thousand Marines. They were among the finest colonels in the corps. Mattis, time and again, had stressed that speed was of the essence. Now the colonel in charge of RCT-1 had stopped at the bridge. Momentum was lost as wild rumors swept through the column, claiming sixty Marines had been killed.

Ray and I parked next to the colonel's vehicle and listened as his subordinate commanders asked for direction. The colonel had gone days without sleep. He was so exhausted that he kept nodding off, jerking awake, and muttering befuddled responses. Brigadier General John Kelly, the Assistant Division Commander, rushed up and got the regiment moving again. A few days later, the regimental commander again hesitated to push his troops forward. Logical thinking crumbles after thirty-six hours without sleep. Twice the colonel had driven himself over the edge of rationality; he was literally too tired to think. For failing to keep up the pace, Mattis relieved him. He was the only Marine regimental commander ever to be removed from command in battle.

Each day, the long column steadily advanced. As we drove along, I felt pity for the corpses in shot-up cars strewn along the highway, men slumped over steering wheels and women in bloody burkas, some holding crushed children. They were on the wrong road at the wrong time, bumping into vehicle-mounted machine gunners concerned that any approaching car was driven by a suicide bomber. While the response was necessary, the results were tragic.

As on every battlefield, we saw good and bad tactical decisions. One day, we were on a recon flight with Kelly. As our Huey skimmed over the rooftop of a farmhouse—*bang! bang! bang!*—three heavy slugs flew by a few feet below our craft. The pilot banked steeply and we roared back over the rooftop, seeing a woman hanging laundry and a teenage boy running away from the handles of a massive anti-aircraft gun. With one press of a button, the pilot could obliterate the roof.

"Don't fire," Kelly said. "We're the only chopper in the area. Tell the infantry to secure that house."

Within an hour, the anti-aircraft gun was captured. Due to John Kelly's restraint, there were no casualties.

* * *

Conversely, another time we had parked our Nissan next to five armored vehicles keeping watch over a canal. Ray and I plunged in to wash off twelve days of grime. As we were getting out, a civilian water truck drove up to the far bank, about two hundred meters away. An older man and his young assistant got out and started walking toward the water. *Brrppp!*—a heavy machine gun opened up. Dust flew from the shirt of the older man who staggered and fell face-first. Within a second, the younger man was also struck down. Then a light machine gun fired, the bullets striking the two inert bodies, raising more puffs of dust. That's called "dusting off." In ten seconds, Ray morphed from a journalist into a furious Marine general with years of combat experience.

"Cease fire!" Ray screamed. "Cease fire! They're no goddamn threat!"

A machine gunner inside one of the vehicles had fired at what he thought might be an enemy. Until the mid-twenties, the human brain is not fully shaped. Teenagers have synapses that don't always close properly. Any teenager, Marine or not, advancing on a confused battlefield with a lethal weapon must be supervised like a hawk.

* * *

On the fourteenth day, we joined a battalion of nine hundred Marines mounted in two dozen massive amphibious vehicles. They were set to cut across the fields in single file on a night march so the enemy could not see them. The colonel in charge gave us a set of night-vision goggles and a handheld radio. We took position in the middle of the line.

What a mistake! Within minutes, the tracks of the amtracs in front of us raised dust so thick Ray could only see a car length. If he sped up, we would smash into the thirty-ton vehicle ahead of us. If he slowed, the one behind us would crush us like a beer can. Ray snarled, gripped the wheel, and for the next half-hour, we sweated, swore, and prayed. The Marines, surprised we survived, dubbed the Nissan "the yellow submarine," a play on the Beatles' smash hit.

* * *

There were a few sharp firefights. On the sixteenth day, we joined a tank battalion about to advance the final thirty miles into Baghdad. At dawn, we headed up a straight two-lane highway, our yellow Nissan midway in a long line of tanks and armored vehicles. As we passed a palm grove, a deafening cascade of Saggers—Russian anti-tank missiles—roared overhead, exploding far away.

Shortly after, we rolled past a sprawling military base. On both sides, the Iraqis had dug in behind earthen berms, with oil burning in the ditches in front of them to obscure our fire. They were sticking their rifles blindly over their parapets, not exposing their heads yet seeming oblivious to the dust giving away their positions. The tanks were returning fire and had zapped a few vehicles, with ammo popping off. Engine parts, unexploded ordnance, and torn tires were strewn on the highway, harmless to the sixty-ton leviathan in front of us but certain to blow out our tires. I snapped photos as we kept pace with the tank in front of us. Ray was weaving right and left. To any Iraqi poking his head up, our yellow submarine had to be a mirage. A rocket grenade zipped past.

"For God's sake, don't stop!" I yelled.

"I'm not an idiot!" Ray snapped.

Driving under fire in our "yellow submarine."

The tank slowed, searching for the target. Its barrel cranked toward the trench line. "Here it comes!" Ray yelled as we both ducked behind the windshield. *Wham!* The overpressure from the 120-mm shell lifted our Nissan off the road, shattered a side window, and split the windshield. Ray drove on, swerving around debris as the run-and-gun assault continued, mile after mile.

By dusk, the armored column had reached a canal on the edge of Baghdad. Lieutenant Brian McPhillips, in a Humvee behind us, had been mortally wounded. He, I, and the regimental colonel Joe Dunford (later the Chairman of the Joint Chiefs of Staff), were all graduates of Boston College High School. The youngest of the three of us was the first to die. Also killed was First Sergeant Edward Smith, with whom we had shared a plastic-food dinner the night before. Ed had extended his enlistment to stay with his company for the invasion.

With the fight over, Ray and I sat on the hood of our yellow Nissan. "Good thing they weren't North Viets," Ray said. "We would've been pasted." The North Vietnamese were the world's finest light infantry. When they dug in, it was like fighting a badger with your bare hands.

Overhearing us, Marines who had just lost two of their own were rightly furious. Each war has its own dynamic. The uniformed Iraqi military was no match for the US military. Consequently, in stand-up battle, our casualties were much lighter than in Vietnam. That's no solace, though. As General Bob Barrow, a Marine commandant who fought in WWII, Korea, and Vietnam, told me, "Bing, I've never seen a crowded battlefield." If you're on the lines in any war, you run the risk of paying the price. There's no such thing as a "light war" to those in it. We should not have said a word.

That evening, as usual, I looked around for a soft spot to scrape out my hip hole. The secret to sleeping on the ground is to put your Camelbak water bag under your head as a pillow and dig a shallow hole for your hip. I was walking up an embankment when I heard a slight whoosh. Instantly, the hair on my neck stood up like a startled dog. *Wham! Wham!* Two artillery shells slammed into the other side of the slope, showering me with only dirt. Surviving takes luck.

We had reached the outskirts of Baghdad, on the far side of what was called the Diyala Canal.

But the Iraqis had blown a large hole in the center of the trestle bridge, preventing the vehicles from crossing. Ray and I were chatting with the lead company at the bridge when General Mattis (left below) walked by us to survey the gap.

Major General Jim Mattis (left) at Diyala Bridge.

A minute later, a shock wave buffeted us, followed by a sharp *bang!* and chunks of metal thudding down. An artillery shell had hit fifty meters away. With a random shot, the Iraqis had almost taken out the Marine commander. It ripped apart the amphibious vehicle behind us. Killed instantly were Corporal Martin Antonio Medellin and Lance Corporal Andrew Julian Aviles. Aged eighteen, Aviles was the youngest to die in the invasion.

Rather than stay exposed to fire, the Marines immediately threw a few planks across the gap in the bridge. One by one, they scampered across, not looking at the boulders seventy feet below. When it was my turn, I took my time crossing. I didn't want Ray to end our book writing with me breaking my neck because I hadn't walked straight.

* * *

Crossing the Diyala Bridge.

Inside Baghdad, the Iraqi army units quickly crumbled. On the 9th of April, Ray and I watched as Marines attached cables to a twenty-foot metal statue of Saddam and hauled it down. In three weeks, the invasion was over. Saddam was in hiding, his reign ended. No WMD—the reason for the invasion—were found. Saddam had pretended they existed to deter his enemies and he lost his bluff. Civilians swarmed like locusts into the government buildings and the wealthy homes of officials. Chaos reigned. The White House, Pentagon and State Department had spent a year planning a successful blitzkrieg but had no plan what to do after that. General Mattis and the other commanders had no instructions about what they were to do.

The shooting, however, had stopped and the war seemed over. Ray and I returned to the States in April and wrote our book about the invasion, entitled *The March Up*. In its chapters, we chronicled day by day the mounted, air-ground, rapid maneuver warfare in which American forces excel.

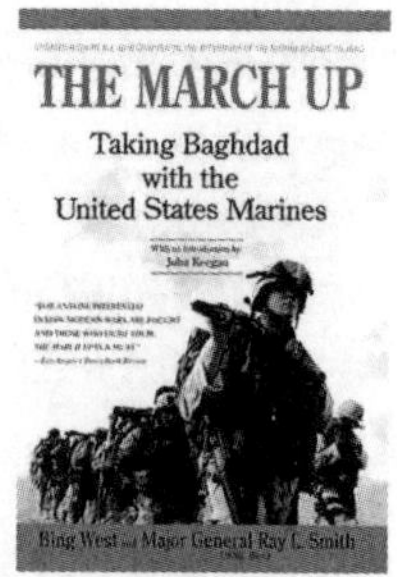

* * *

In the late summer of 2003, Ray resumed his business and I returned to Iraq to see how things were going. President George W. Bush had appointed a personal envoy—Ambassador L. Paul "Jerry" Bremer—to run the country. Inside a guarded enclave in Baghdad called the Green Zone, Bremer presided over hundreds of contractors, aid workers, diplomats, and soldiers who were sleeping in double-decker cots, snoring, farting, and cursing. Activity was frenetic and disorganized.

I quickly hitched a ride south, where I visited seven Marine battalions, each stationed in a Shiite city. Each battalion commander was acting as the de facto mayor. They had assumed the chores our State Department officials should have performed. With Bremer linked directly to Bush, Secretary of State Colin Powell, smarting about the WMD intelligence failure, and his chameleon deputy, Richard Armitage, had distanced the State Department from the war.

In the city of Al Diwaniyah, I watched hundreds of former Iraqi soldiers in civilian clothes standing in a pay line. Rather than be decimated by the invading force, most of the Iraqi army had shucked their uniforms and run away. The US military was providing the soldiers with a final mustering-out payment, hoping the cash would prevent desperate looting. When Mattis arrived, they stood at attention. The Marine battalion commander explained that the soldiers were anxious to serve. Mattis decided to cull the ranks to create a security force, with its officers chosen by us.

However, Bremer summarily abolished the entire Iraqi Army and restricted former members of Saddam's Ba'athist Party from holding government jobs, although they had the requisite experience. This meant that 150,000 US and coalition soldiers were responsible for providing both security and de facto governance over ten million Kurds, ten million Sunnis, and twenty million Shiites—three sects that loathed one another.

On one dawn raid, I went with recon Marines mounted in three armored trucks. A half mile outside the gate—*wham! wham! wham!*—we were hit by three roadside bombs. The artillery shells, dug into the roadside and detonated by a battery wire running to a hidden sentinel, exploded in between our vehicles. We were rocked around, but no one was injured. The attackers escaped and we hurried on to our objective, a mansion overlooking the Euphrates. As we screeched to a halt, the hunted—one of Saddam's generals—leaped off the back balcony into the river. We fruitlessly searched the bulrushes. He either escaped or drowned in the three-knot current.

Secretary of Defense Donald Rumsfeld had referred to a few remaining "dead-enders." But dead-enders don't set off strings of bombs to kill you. With Syria providing sanctuary for die-hard Saddam supporters and Islamist terrorists, an insurgency was blossoming.

✶ ✶ ✶

I returned to the States. A few months later, Rumsfeld and Deputy Secretary Paul Wolfowitz asked me to go back for a third embed as part of a team to assess the security conditions. After three weeks traveling across Iraq, our team concluded that Bremer, who reported only to Bush, wielded the authority to make decisions about security. Our military was responsible for carrying out his decisions. We recommended the military, not Bremer, be given the authority to make the decisions. The White House made that amendment. It was far from sufficient.

* * *

In the spring of 2004, I returned for my fourth embed. Had I not witnessed it firsthand, I would not have believed the disaster that had unfolded in less than a year, The primary locus of the rebellion was Anbar Province, west of Baghdad. Two million tribal Sunnis lived there in a dozen cities along the Euphrates River that snaked northwesterly to the Jordanian and Syrian border. In March, four American contractors were driving through the restive city of Fallujah when they were ambushed. Their bodies were burned and strung from a trestle bridge, with the gruesome video shown globally.

Mattis advised eliminating the ringleaders, while working with local Sunni forces to settle down the city. In anger, Bush, Powell, and Rumsfeld, supported by Bremer, ignored his recommendation. Reinforcing each other's indignation, the National Security Council unanimously agreed to order Mattis, with three thousand available troops, to seize the city of 300,000. Marines, Bush declared, were "perfect for kicking ass."

The Marines had to fight both youths defending their city, and Al Qaeda forces led by the arch-terrorist Abu Musab al-Zarqawi, who was hiding there and dispatching suicide bombers who killed hundreds of Shiites. His goal was to provoke Shiites to exact revenge upon the Sunnis. After both sects exhausted themselves in civil war, his organization—called Al Qaeda in Iraq or AQI—would emerge triumphant and establish a ninth-century caliphate.

Not wanting to miss the battle, I flew over, and in early April, I joined Lieutenant Colonel Bryan McCoy's battalion that was already halfway across the city. His squads were advancing abreast on adjoining streets, not letting shooters hit them from the flanks. On Easter Sunday, I was talking with McCoy when a Marine behind us climbed up a light tower to look around. He was shot and killed. We were held up by a sniper firing from a minaret. An F-18 was circling overhead. "Shack it," McCoy radioed. The minaret crumbled and the grunts moved forward. They systematically squeezed Zarqawi's terrorists toward a last stand along the bank of the Euphrates River.

The next day, McCoy told me the high command had ordered the Marines to halt and negotiate. Al Jazeera had been posting false images daily of horrendous damage. This included a picture of dead babies that would bring tears to a rock. They had supposedly been killed by artillery. That Mattis had brought no artillery to Iraq didn't matter. Bush and his top officials, including Bremer, lost their nerve and called off the attack. It was like the owner of a football team, watching from his skybox, telling his team to give the ball to the other side.

For the next two weeks, a steaming Mattis haggled with negotiators who were fronting for Zarqawi, while the fighting continued on the frontlines. I joined Captain Doug Zembiec on the roof of an apartment building. Doug had a manic grin, and the troops called him "the Lion of Fallujah." He showed me his map schema to seize another six to eight city blocks (at least six hundred buildings) with his 130-man company. He was happy to see me, because he wanted three tanks and thought I could pry them out of Mattis. If I could, he promised to take me elk hunting with him and his dad. (I wasn't crazy enough to mention it to Mattis.)

All that night, mortar shells dropped randomly around. On the floor below us, the Marines had placed a mattress over the flowery China in the dining room. We could hear the imams over the loudspeakers in minarets exhorting the people to fight. The Marines responded by blasting hip-hop music and the genuinely scary growl of the monster in the movie *Predator*. Unable to sleep, we talked for hours. Doug's enthusiasm was infectious.

"I'm never so alive as in a firefight," he said, looking up at the flares. "Time slows down for me. I can visualize it all, sense what they're going to do next."

From our vantage point the next morning, we could see for half a mile down a broad avenue dotted with burned-out cars. Doug was like a tour guide explaining the sights.

Doug Zembiec, "The Lion of Fallujah."

A sniper pointed out a boy toting a mortar shell across the street. "I let the kids go," he said. "I red light the adult idiots. That telephone pole is my aim point." He gave me his spotting scope. I dialed in the pole about seven hundred meters away and saw a body lying next to it.

"When I see a squirter lugging ammo," the sniper said, "I squeeze at that pole and he runs into the bullet. Some collapse, most stagger away."

"The impact doesn't knock them off their feet?"

"Nah, that only happens in Hollywood."

After a month of empty negotiations, the White House ordered the Marines to turn the city over to the terrorists. I accompanied Mattis and a handful of his guards to a ceremony at city hall. Waiting for us was the wispy-bearded Imam Janabi, who was Zarqawi's "spiritual advisor." Mattis hoped a gunfight would erupt. The meeting was tense and brief. Mattis insulted him, calling him a terrorist. But Janabi, despite a temperamental reputation, glanced away. No fight broke out. With no choice, a tight-lipped Mattis and his Marines drove out of the city, leaving the terrorists in charge.

Between 2003 and 2012, I made fifteen trips to Iraq. Fallujah in May 2004 was the low point. It is hard to exaggerate the severity of that setback. Mattis intended to destroy Zarqawi and the Al Qaeda movement before it gained momentum, but the White House had lost its nerve. Our top-level leaders violated the basic tenet of war-fighting: Once committed, finish the fight. One month of incoherence by our civilian–military hierarchy caused an escalation of the war.

$$* * *$$

I went back for the second battle of Fallujah in the fall of 2004. The terrorists had controlled the city for five months, dispatching suicide bombers to blow up Shiite mosques, murdering thousands. Abetted by Iran, radical Shiites responded by forming militias to attack Sunni neighborhoods, initiating the civil war Zarqawi and Al Qaeda desired. After Bush was reelected in November 2004, the Iraqi government gave the OK to invade Fallujah a second time. Seven battalions assaulted the city, destroying the insurgent force, estimated to number two thousand, inside three weeks.

As the battle began, I visited with a Marine unit called The Watchdogs. It controlled several drones, each mounted with a forward-looking infrared (FLIR) camera, a high-resolution day camera, and a digital downlink to an artillery battery. At night, I watched as video from the FLIR showed the houses in sharp contrast to the palm trees in the courtyards. We watched a line of white ghosts snaking around the trees.

"A dozen muj on the move," the camera operator said.

In the ops center, an operator glanced at the numbers showing on a corner of the video, typed in the grid location, and passed the data to a huge four-engine C-130 aircraft circling overhead, armed with machine guns, an artillery canon, and a huge infrared spotlight. The plane fired an artillery shell, and on the video screen, a large black spot blossomed. Four figures went down, and one survivor staggered away. The plane fired again. A second ink spot enveloped the lone survivor. I was witnessing the advent of the drone warfare that is now a staple on all battlefields.

The next afternoon, I watched three insurgents firing a mortar from a courtyard in a vivid color video. One adjusted the aiming device on the tube, while another draped sandbags over the tube's bipod legs to stabilize it. After the third fighter dropped a shell down the tube, they scampered back to the concealment of a domed, two-story house. The ops center called for an F-18 strike.

While this was going on, a van drove up to the house. The driver unloaded trays of flat bread. On battlefields around the world, shooting dies down at dinner time. Humans gather to eat the evening meal with others, no matter the setting. Sure enough, about a dozen insurgents popped out of various hiding places and entered the house. The F-18 pilot radioed that he was aligning his sights on the mortar tube.

"No, no, no," the Marines in the ops center shouted. "The house! Hit the house!"

A minute later, the dome disappeared in a black blob. As the smoke drifted away and black bits of burned debris lay scattered across the courtyard, a sole black figure staggered out. A second missile obliterated him and the mortar tube.

The city had absorbed sledgehammer blows by tanks as well as air. Out on the wrecked streets, Marines and Army soldiers advanced by squads day after day, searching every house. Inside about one in sixty houses, Islamists were barricaded, waiting to kill before dying. The squad I accompanied advanced warily, never knowing where the next fight would erupt. You looked for shit piles near a house as a warning sign.

Fallujah.

The battalion commander, Lieutenant Colonel Pat Malay, drove up to talk with the squad leader. As his Humvee passed a junk-strewn alley, a volley of AK rounds broke out. A second Humvee rushed up, and inside half a minute, four insurgents were killed. Malay shot one of the four.

"It's a good day when you get into it," Corporal Michael Yerena, the vehicle commander in the second Humvee, said to me. "You feel you've earned your pay."

On the eastern bank of the Euphrates in the Jolan district, the grunts had broken into a dumpy warehouse. Malay brought me in to take a look. We tramped down a narrow passageway behind the foreman's cluttered office and emerged inside Zarqawi's concealed lair. On one yellowish wall hung the Al Qaeda black flag. Lying on the floor nearby were two theater spotlights, and off to one side was a table strewn with pieces of computer junk. Here was where Zarqawi had beheaded the young American civilian, Nicholas Berg, in May 2004. The gruesome video was posted online. The cloying stink of death filled the room. Malay gestured to a small cell with iron bars and chains anchored into the wall. A legless, blackened corpse, half-burned, lay crumbled in the dirt.

I had seen death up close in battle. The stickiness of the sopping blood, its sugary yuck smell, the lips seeming to turn blue, the finality, the sudden swarm of green-head flies. This was different. This was evil, not battle. The Marines had no idea who he was. For what possible purpose had the poor man been tortured? Dusty daylight filtered through a small, dirty window, glass still intact. In a park about a hundred meters away, I saw a brightly colored merry-go-round. Printed in red letters were the words United States, a USAID gift from an earlier time. I wondered if children had heard screams from the warehouse.

Falujah Merry-Go-Round.

The second battle for Fallujah yielded no improvement in the war. Dressed as a woman, Zarqawi escaped. It would be another year before he was killed by an air strike. By then his terrorist network had metastasized across Iraq.

Returning to Newport, I wrote the book, *No True Glory: A Frontline Account of the Battle for Fallujah.* It covered my several embeds on the frontlines plus a thousand interviews, from grunts to the White House. The book explained how a major battle unfolds, contrasting the bravery on the fighting fields with the errant decisions at the top.

* * *

Fallujah was over in a blink of history, a faraway and inconclusive fight two decades ago. In the spring of 2004, President Bush and his national security advisers—civilian and military—had lost their nerve due to adverse publicity and pulled out the Marines. The city became a sanctuary for Al Qaeda to boost recruiting and from which to attack the Shiites. By the time Fallujah was again seized and occupied at the end of 2004, AQI had succeeded in igniting a sectarian civil war.

* * *

Our soldiers were fighting two invisible mafias, Sunni Islamists led by Al Qaeda zealots and Shiite militias supported by Iran. I had viewed the snuff films of Shiites tortured by Saddam's enforcers. One showed a man tied backward on a donkey trotting around a crowded village square. On the black-and-white film, his naked back displayed the crisscrosses from whipping. In another video, men grotesquely festooned in Superman T-shirts were forced to leap off roofs, grasping for tree branches before landing with broken legs and backs. The Shiites, now in control of the government and oil revenues, were eager to exact revenge upon the hated Sunnis.

As I embedded with dozens of units in 2005 and 2006, the combat took on a sameness. Iraq was a war fought by moving around in vehicles. The terrain is flat, with stony deserts, scrub land, and squishy marshes outside the Fertile Crescent between the Euphrates and Tigris rivers. More than half the population lives in cities and the towns on the highways connecting the cities. Military convoys and Humvees were on the move twenty-four hours a day. Both the Sunni and Shiite factions wore civilian clothes and mingled among civilians. Our troops on mounted and foot patrols had no way of identifying them.

The enemy became skilled at making improvised explosive devices. Explosives, blasting caps, and batteries were readily available. Half of all friendly casualties were inflicted by IEDs. They were hidden behind signs, in garbage heaps, under floors in houses, in culverts, parked cars, and in everyday pieces of trash. Anything that provided concealment could blow up in your face.

I embedded several times in Ramadi, Anbar's capital. It was worse than Fallujah, its violent neighbor twenty miles south down the highway. Ramadi was a total wreck, with insurgents firing nightly from apartments occupied by families and inserting IEDs on every street. When I accompanied a mounted patrol, we had driven less than half a mile before I snapped this photo of an IED in the middle of the street, wrapped in tan paper with white bands.

IED in a tan cardboard box with white wrapping in the middle of the road.

Had we driven past half an hour later when it was dark, we would not have seen it in time. Two engineers joined us, equipped with a small robot to attach a blasting cap to the IED and return to our position. A radio signal would then detonate the IED. However, as soon as the robot stopped alongside the IED, a hidden insurgent sent his signal, blowing up both the IED and the robot. The engineer next to me let loose a string of expletives.

"Freddie [the robot] cost us ninety thousand dollars," he said. "That IED cost them nine dollars."

On one occasion in Baghdad, our Humvee was splashing through a deep puddle. In a roadside shop next to us, a blacksmith was straightening a bicycle fender. As we drew abreast of him, our Humvee suddenly jumped a few feet into the air. An IED had hit the vehicle a few feet in front of us, ripping out the engine. The soldiers inside were not hurt because the shrapnel was forced sideways.

The blacksmith had been knocked off his feet and began screaming. Our medic quickly bound his left bicep, but he had lost his forearm. In shock, he lay on his side looking at his blood. Did he know the explosive was hidden in the puddle? Probably. The IED was intended for us, not for him. But he hadn't backed far enough away.

Another time, our three Humvees took fire from a crowded building in Ramadi. The Marines stopped and tumbled out, spoiling for a fight. Iraqi males were fleeing in all directions. A bullet hit one mid-thigh. As a corpsman wrapped a tourniquet, he shook his head in frustration. The femoral artery had been cut and the skin was swelling like a fried sausage. He was bleeding to death and his eyes were wide, shocked and begging.

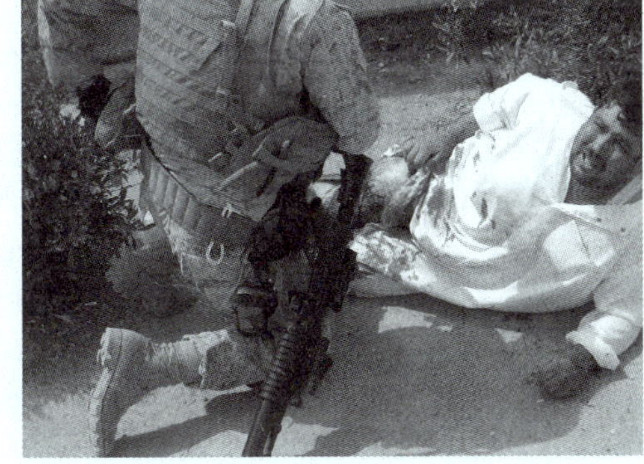

When you are looking at a body already stiff, you can erect a mental shield. It's different to see life leaving as the blood and oxygen leak out.

For our grunts in 2005 to 2006, the daily routine seemed similar to the state police in, say, New York. Patrols, either in Humvees or afoot, settled into six-hour shifts, waiting for the unseen IED to explode or the hidden enemy to shoot first. Sometimes there was a small exchange of fire; usually, there was no shooting. Then back to comfortable FOBs—forward operating bases. Due to digital communications, chats with the families were nightly. The troops ate not in mess halls but in D-Facs, or dining facilities. Cheerful workers from Bangladesh offered a choice of three entrées and ten flavors of ice cream. The cost per meal (in 2025 dollars) was $40, or $120 for a soldier who ate three meals a day. At night, our soldiers slept on cots with mattresses in air-conditioned barracks.

It seemed police routine. Then, on a boring patrol, *WHAM!* your Humvee is blown up. Our soldiers died in numbers inconceivable in police work in the States. IEDs accounted for 50 percent of our fatalities. Iran provided both the Sunni terrorists and the Shiite militias with a vicious IED that accounted for more than four hundred American deaths. Particularly frustrating was the revolving door of a broken Iraqi justice system. Time and again, those arrested for emplacing IEDs were let loose from prison within a few months. In a country racked with killings, proportionately far fewer Iraqis were convicted of violent crimes than in the US.

I attended briefings where our generals listened while fifty to one hundred officers clicked on their laptops to show masses of disparate data. The command in Baghdad concocted a dizzying color-coded chart that lumped together electrification, air conditioning, clean water, highway projects, insurgent attacks, sanitation, assassinations, and roadside bombs. How anyone was to make sense of all the variables was mystifying. This illustrated the confusion about the mission. After the State Department and USAID stepped to the sidelines, the military had to provide and manage development projects.

According to Army and Marine doctrine, the troops were "expected to be nation-builders as well as warriors." Our generals embraced the novel theory that benevolence, cash, and infrastructure projects were essential military tasks in the prosecution of a war to impose democracy. One general bragged about laying kilometers of sewer pipes in Sadr City, the stronghold of Shiite militias. The sewers did not flush out the poison of extremism. The general's successor had to launch an assault inside Sadr to break the power of the Shiite militias.

I listened to company commanders dutifully explain how they gave away more than $25,000 a month. This money did not persuade people to betray the mafia living among them, ready to slice the throats of anyone who pointed them out. The generals at the top assumed that eighteen-year-old privates could do the job that State Department professionals had walked away from. Nonetheless, everywhere I went, there were our grunts, standing forth, sticking at it. They didn't retreat into cynicism. They kept plugging away, patrolling every day.

Typical street patrol.

By 2006, the Shiite militias were pushing from the south into sprawling Baghdad. These vigilantes were forcing the Sunnis to relinquish their homes. In a Bagdad suburb, I accompanied Lieutenant Sam Crabtree of the First Cavalry Division, who was responding to shots fired by a local gang. We knocked at the door of an attractive suburban two-story house with a rose garden in the courtyard. A nervous Shiite woman, with no identification card and three shy children, greeted us. Our interpreter pointed to pictures of a handsome Iraqi Air Force captain. The woman said she didn't know him. When she arrived a few hours ago, a wailing Sunni woman and her children had just been thrown out of the house, with the Shiite militia throwing stones at them. The new "owner" stood frozen while the children whimpered. Crabtree had no legal authority, and the district chief was a Shiite factotum. Frustrated, he left.

We drove to an adjoining street to record the location of a corpse rolled in a rug and dumped on top of a garbage heap. Every night, men were snatched from their homes and tortured or shot. Two blocks on, he pointed to another body, lying uncovered in a ditch. Such was the daily turbulence and fear that it would be days before either body was collected. The traditional Muslim one-day burial was broken. Neighborhood cohesion had collapsed. In the steady displacement of the Sunnis, the Shiite central government was complicit, both actively and by silent toleration.

Another time, two MPs (military police) sneaked me into a Baghdad prison. A stone archway led to a line of barred, windowless cells with no electricity or plumbing. I thought there should be a plaque: *Abandon hope, all ye who enter here*. The guards carried out a haggard man in his twenties, with a scraggly beard and a resigned expression. He would hang at dawn. He wasn't shackled. His feet, wrapped in rags, flopped at odd angles. The guards said he had jumped out a window when police, alerted by neighbors, had broken up a raucous, late-night party.

Responding to a rap on his ankle, he told his story in a flat, detached tone. He said he spent his days wandering the streets, penniless. A "religious" man convinced him that as a Sunni, it was his duty before Allah to take vengeance upon the Shiites. After being handed a pistol, he boarded a bus, told the Sunnis to get off, and robbed the Shiites. When he said no more, a guard prodded him.

"I shot them," he screeched.

How many? "Eleven."

A few days later, the "religious man" pointed out a policeman in civilian clothes. To earn two hundred dollars, all the killer had to do was shoot the cop. This the killer did. Again, he fell silent, only responding when a guard glared at him. He said he also killed the policeman's eight-year-old daughter and stole his car. Once he was paid, he threw a drunken party that was busted by the police. Searched at the station, he turned over the car keys, with a rabbit's foot attached. The precinct captain recognized the rabbit's foot. It was his brother's car keys.

The condemned prisoner related all this in a monotone, eyes black and blank. I was looking at a man who chose to die, beyond redemption. No inflection in his voice, no sign of remorse, sorrow, or regret for what he had done. You kill, you get caught, you hang. That's life.

That's what happened when Islamist fanatics fastened their grip on shiftless youths with no character. By paying a pittance, the terrorists turned them into robotic killers. As a killer sinks deeper into evil, murdering becomes habitual. It's as if he's thinking, *Since I'm going to burn forever, I might as well enjoy this moment.* The most zealous Islamists believed they were creating a medieval caliphate. Many of their followers, like this killer awaiting hanging, believed in nothing.

✷ ✷ ✷

Not all our units were well-led. On one routine sweep, I joined a Marine battalion. We drove in single file, and when fired upon, the entire file stopped and waited while the battalion commander and his bodyguard ran after the shooter. The door in my Humvee was secured with a piece of rope. The driver objected to my getting out because, with an open door, he might be shot.

I ate lunch with a company commander in his plywood hooch. As we munched on flat bread spread with peanut butter, the captain explained he had a situation on his hands. The night before, a suspect had been interrogated by local police, with some Marines looking on. The suspect had died. The captain had stashed him in the freezer until investigators arrived. I didn't stay for the ice cream dessert.

* * *

By 2006, the US high command had concluded that American soldiers, not trained as police, were blundering and causing resentment. Supposedly, American soldiers were an "antibody" rejected by the Iraqi culture. In Baghdad, US soldiers were pulled off the streets and into large bases. In Anbar Province to the west, the Marines refused to pull back. But they, too, seemed to be accomplishing nothing.

In Fallujah, I attended a dinner at a Sunni sheikh's compound guarded by his close relatives. Sitting on soft rugs on the close-cropped lawn, the sheikh protested that he'd like to get back to normal living. Cooperate with the Marines, though, and he'd be killed. In three years, Al Qaeda had murdered hundreds of Sunni sheikhs and intimidated the rest. Some fled to Jordan. Others, like our host, hunkered down, politely refusing offers of protection.

The next night, I accompanied a mounted patrol that zigzagged through the giant concrete barriers erected to deflect the blasts of IEDs. We hadn't been out an hour when an IED exploded harmlessly in front of us. The patrol returned to base. There was no sense in continuing. We were sitting ducks out there, driving around blind.

That summer, I visited a battalion outside Ramadi. One day, the grunts, through binoculars, identified a known Al Qaeda operative shopping in a bazaar. He was hobbling along on crutches. Within ten minutes, a squad had rushed into the crowded market. However, the suspect had disappeared; not one of the shoppers questioned had seen a man on crutches.

That night, I accompanied a patrol through the paddies adjoining the marketplace. When the platoon commander was beyond hearing distance, the grunts complained.

"This is a waste of time," one said. "We never get anywhere."

"We're chasing ghosts," another said.

Nonetheless, the grunts stayed at it, plodding along while bitching. The repeated explosions of IEDs and the standoffishness of the Sunni sheikhs attested to the power of Al Qaeda hiding in the shadows. Radio intercepts were rare, and the local police reported nothing. In the summer of 2006, a Marine intelligence report, leaked to the press, concluded that the war was not being won. A stalemate existed, with no indications of progress. In Sunni areas, Al Qaeda was sheltered by communities that refused to point them out. In Baghdad and its environs, Shiite militias, protected by the central government, were pushing Sunni families out of their homes. The country was falling apart.

* * *

Then came an unanticipated, precipitous, and war-changing cultural shift. After murdering a leading family of the Abu Risha tribe outside Ramadi, Al Qaeda lured a surviving young sheikh, Abdul Sattar, into an ambush. Sattar radioed to the US base for help, and tanks roared out to rescue him. Sattar then chose to throw in with the Americans. He called together his tribesmen, urging them to join what he called "the Anbar Awakening." The Sunni tribes, he argued, had to awaken to the reality that Al Qaeda intended to crush and rule them. Al Qaeda, not the Americans, were the real enemy in Anbar.

"When American soldiers are in the vicinity," he counseled, "point out the terrorists hiding in civilian clothes among you. The Americans will take care of them." This was the alliance generals Jim Mattis and John Kelly had tried to pursue three years earlier. Since then, the Marines had plugged away at wooing over the tribes, absorbing rebuff after rebuff. While the pivot of the Sunni tribes seemed to happen suddenly under Sattar, it was actually based on years of persistent patrolling and patient outreach.

A thoughtful man with piercing black eyes and a trim beard, I liked Sattar for his directness.

"Why," I asked him, "did it take years of killings and misery before your tribe realized the Americans were your best hope?"

"You Americans," he replied, "could not convince us. We had to decide for ourselves."

Sheikh Abdul Sattar led the Sunni "awakening" that won the war (for a while).

He trusted America and distrusted what he called "the Persian government of Maliki." Sattar's uprising spread swiftly, as other tribes "awakened" to take back their fiefdoms (not least because they didn't want Sattar gaining too much influence).

In early December 2006, I was visiting Iraq as Mattis's (now a three-star general) guest. To my surprise, we flew to Habbineah, a small town between Ramadi and Fallujah. My son, Owen, was leading an advisory team there. Mattis asked about the awakening. Owen said that local tribesmen had nailed a list to the mosque door, naming about sixty terrorists. At a gas station where dozens of cars waited in a queue, a terrorist was clubbed to death as onlookers cheered. Within hours, the other terrorists had fled town.

Lieutenant General Jim Mattis and author in Habbineah.

After seeing Owen, Mattis and I went on to Ramadi. Colonel Sean MacFarland, in charge of the city, told us that the awakening had changed the battlefield. His advisor on tribal matters was Army Captain Travis Patriquin, who energetically urged US units of all sizes to work with the tribes. He had created a stick-man PowerPoint briefing that showed, step by step, why the tribes were the key to winning the war. He joked with me that the cartoonish stick-man style allowed Marines to grasp the idea. Mattis congratulated Mac-Farland. Now that the tribes had come over, Al Qaeda had no place to hide. Mattis told me the war in Anbar had been won.

While MacFarland and Mattis talked, I accepted Major Megan McClung's invite to lunch. She was the Public Affairs (press) officer, a serious runner pushing for marathons to be held inside the sprawling US bases. Pert and smiling, she joked that, given my advanced age, I should take her on my patrols since she was fit enough to carry me out. A few days later, a massive IED killed McClung, Patriquin, and Specialist Vincent Pomante.

* * *

At the same time, in December 2006, Bush was under intense pressure. The Democrats, with majorities in the Senate and House, had turned against the war. The State Department urged an honorable withdrawal, with many policymakers in favor of restricting US forces in Baghdad to isolated bases. The National Security Advisor, Stephen Hadley, quietly visited Iraq. Upon returning, he told Bush the pendulum was swinging in Anbar, despite reports to the contrary. Instead of seeking a way out, Bush ordered the deployment of thirty thousand more soldiers under a new top commander, Army General David Petraeus. Unlike President Lyndon B. Johnson in Vietnam, Bush wanted to win.

Petraeus bulked up the Army forces in Baghdad and elsewhere, shifting them from their bases into hundreds of outposts. He believed in communicating a few "big ideas," namely, (1) Don't commute to work, stay in the neighborhoods, and (2) Don't patrol alone, include the Iraqis in everything you do. Once positioned among the people, the US Army companies allied with local Sunnis who wanted to duplicate the Anbar Awakening. Working as armed neighborhood watches, they turned against the local Al Qaeda networks. Eventually, Petraeus was paying eighty-five thousand "Sons of Iraq" nested in cities, districts, and villages. No longer able to hide among the people, Al Qaeda's power was broken.

In September 2007, Bush flew to Anbar Province to thank Sattar and the Sunni sheikhs. A few weeks later, Sattar was assassinated by a cousin. Al Qaeda had promised him $5,000 for the murder. After his arrest, he confessed he was never paid.

Still, the war had been won. In 2007, when I embedded with Lieutenant Colonel Ken Adgie's battalion on the outskirts of Baghdad, it had taken us four hours to move two kilometers down the main road, so thick were the IEDs. In 2008, as Ken drove me down that same road, he waved at smiling people. He brought me inside a small store, pointing to its shelves crammed with clothes, canned goods, and farm tools. I thought back to 2004, when Captain Doug Zembiec had proudly shown me a sniper shooting the enemy in Fallujah. Four years later, Ken was proudly showing me a store owner selling shovels and wheelbarrows.

Zembiec wasn't there to congratulate Ken. After Fallujah, he had joined the CIA's Special Activities Division and was shot in 2007 during a night raid in Baghdad. His gravesite at Arlington was close to that of his Naval Academy classmate, Megan McClung.

Iraq hadn't been the joyful and swift liberation the Bush administration had anticipated. But by 2008, the American military had prevailed. During the battle for Fallujah, an Iraqi colonel had pointed at a Marine patrol passing by.

"Americans," he said, "are the strongest tribe."

My third book about Iraq was entitled *The Strongest Tribe*. I described how American grunts had persisted until the Sunni tribes finally swung over. With local intelligence then pouring in, the Sunni terrorists fled to Syria.

Backed by American firepower, Prime Minister Nouri al-Maliki then quashed the radical Iranian-sponsored Shiite militias. He was very much in control. When I interviewed him, I said that in Sunni cities, the garbage heaps were as tall as houses and the women filled water buckets from rusty pipes. In contrast, Shiite cities in the south were benefiting from government funds. Maliki replied that the Sunnis were receiving what they needed. End of discussion.

The US command knew Maliki was a sectarian Shiite. However, a web of US advisors at all levels in the Iraqi army and agencies provided the means of detecting and stifling the worst instincts of Maliki and his crew. Through 2010, our troops nurtured a fragile peace. It seemed the strongest tribe (America) had prevailed, and that a democracy was emerging in the Middle East.

After 2011, I did not return to Iraq. The unnecessary and tragic end to our involvement in Iraq is addressed in the next chapter.

Iraq Policy: Why We Lost

Explaining in 2003 why the United States invaded Iraq, President George W. Bush declared, *"I will not leave the American people at the mercy of the Iraqi dictator and his weapons."*[1] Saddam Hussein was toppled in three weeks. No WMD were found. President Bush then changed the mission to democratic nation-building. *"Iraqi democracy will succeed,"* he declared, *"and that success will send forth the news, from Damascus to Teheran, that freedom can be the future of every nation. The establishment of a free Iraq at the heart of the Middle East will be a watershed event in the global democratic revolution."*

The problem was that neither the military nor the diplomats knew how to accomplish that staggering mission. In violent Ramadi in 2004, I asked Army Lieutenant General Thomas Metz, then the deputy commander in Iraq, what defined success. He cited South Korea, where it had taken half a century for democracy to take root—and where thirty thousand American troops were still stationed seventy-five years later.

Bush soon elevated democratization into a regional doctrine. *"Afghanistan and Iraq will lead that part of the world to democracy,"* he promised. *"They are going to be the catalyst to change the Middle East and the world."*[2] But there was no plan spelling out the resources or time required. Of all the policy mistakes in Iraq and Afghanistan, the fatal one was Bush's failure to grasp and acknowledge that he was binding his successors for decades, with tens of thousands of US troops deployed. Building democratic nations was a political philosophy, not a military mission; South Korea was proof that real democracy demanded fifty or more years to solidify.

Bush was inconsistent about the scale and duration of what he had started. In 2008, he allowed the sectarian Shiite leaders to decide—within three years—whether American forces could remain in Iraq. He knew Prime Minister Nouri al-Maliki was untrustworthy and tied to Iran, yet he gave Maliki the final say. The colossal misstep was first assuming Iraq could become a model democracy and then handing power to a deceiver.

* * *

Our Founding Founders designed checks and balances to protect minorities from majoritarian rule. In Iraq, however, US policymakers created a system that concentrated too much authority in a central government elected by the majority Shiites—disenfranchising Sunni and Kurdish minorities. By late 2004, Iran was funneling $11 million a week to its favored radical Shiite blocs. CIA proposed funding a moderate Iraqi candidate; the United States had done precisely that in Italy, France, and Greece after World War II. But National Security Advisor Condoleezza Rice and Representative Nancy Pelosi objected, calling such aid anti-democratic, and Bush rejected the proposal.[3] Idealism trumped political reality. The Shiite bloc intended to marginalize the Sunnis who had oppressed them for decades.

When Maliki came to power, Bush was warned that he was a vengeful Shiite sectarian. Bush believed that leaders, not cultures, steered nations. Even though intercepts showed Maliki mocking him, Bush thought weekly conversations would change Maliki's character.

By late 2006, Iraq was collapsing. To his credit, Bush did not quit. He surged more troops under a new commander, General David Petraeus. Capitalizing on the Anbar Awakening sparked by Sheikh Abdul Sattar, Petraeus flooded US forces into every Sunni district and funded Sunni "neighborhood watches." Al Qaeda fragmented and fled to Syrian sanctuaries.

Petraeus transformed soldiers into improvised nation-builders. For a brief period, it seemed to work. Sunnis welcomed American patrols because they needed protection from the Shiite government Washington had constructed. The US had stabilized Iraq by toppling Saddam, then shielding Sunnis from the vengeance of newly empowered Shiites—not by building a unified nation.

As the 2011 withdrawal deadline approached, the Pentagon, State Department, and CIA all insisted that Iraq would unravel if US forces left. President Barack Obama and Vice President Joe Biden disagreed. *"All too often our government made decisions based on fear rather than foresight,"* Obama said, criticizing Bush. *"That all too often our government trimmed facts and evidence to fit ideological predispositions."*[4] He ordered a full withdrawal. The decision reflected an ideological view: that the US military was an instrument of imperialism, and the United States had neither the right nor the obligation to remain.

Once US forces departed, Maliki dismantled the Sunni watch groups and stacked the army with cronies, destroying cohesion and morale. Within two years, Al Qaeda—renamed ISIS—poured back from Syria. In 2014, it seized Fallujah, slaughtered the Abu Issa tribe that had led the Anbar Awakening, and overran northern Sunni cities.

Facing state collapse, Iraqi leaders ousted Maliki and begged America to return. Obama sent back advisers, artillery teams, and airpower. They rallied Iraqi forces and pulverized ISIS strongholds. By 2020, with Donald J. Trump in the White House, ISIS remnants were driven back into Syria.

But, like Obama, Trump squandered the gains by pulling US troops out and surrendering American leverage. His isolationism differed from Obama's—Trump was motivated not by anti-imperial philosophy but by anger that America had not "won," blaming "neocons" for endless wars.

Back in 2003, Bush had predicted, *"A new regime in Iraq would serve as a dramatic and inspiring example of freedom for other nations in the region."*[5] By 2025, a corrupt and sectarian Shiite government in Baghdad—too weak to resist Iran—presided over a failed state. Iran, America's sworn enemy, emerged the net victor, and Iraq became its submissive satellite.

The war cost more than seven thousand American service members and contractors killed, and more than a trillion dollars expended.[6] There was no continuity of purpose. Instead, each president contradicted the last: Bush bet his successors would embrace nation-building; Obama rejected the mission without offering an alternative; Trump repeated Obama's withdrawal, forfeiting influence yet again. The result was predictable: Iraq convulsed, Al Qaeda resurged in 2014, and US forces had to reenter—only to depart again.

Iraq was a policy failure, not a battlefield defeat. As Ambassador Eliot Cohen warned, *"Once you go to war, persevere."* Our policymakers did not persevere.

Battle in Afghanistan

On September 11, 2001, Al Qaeda terrorists crashed two passenger planes into the World Trade Center buildings, murdering three thousand civilians. Osama bin Laden had planned the attack in remote Afghanistan, sheltered there by the Taliban government. Within three months, US air strikes had shattered the enemy force. Al Qaeda core fighters fled into the Tora Bora Mountain range. Brigadier General Jim Mattis recommended that his four thousand Marines and Special Forces, already based inside Afghanistan, attack to finish them off. Instead, the US military high command in Tampa, FL, handed off the mission to Afghan warlords. This resulted in Al Qaeda's escape into Pakistan. The failure to employ US forces was described by a *New York Times* reporter as "the gravest error of the war."[1] It would be another twenty years before Al Qaeda as a cohesive military force was stamped out.

Instead of then turning the fractured country over to the United Nations as a protectorate, President George W. Bush changed the US mission from destroying Al Qaeda to building a democratic nation. With soaring mountains in the north and parching deserts in the south, Afghanistan's serrated terrain had for centuries led to isolationism and feuds among its fierce tribes. With the Taliban temporarily in disarray, the United States and the United Nations facilitated the election of erratic Hamid Karzai as the country's president and bestowed lavish aid upon his hand-picked kleptocratic bureaucracy.

Presuming Afghanistan to be stable by 2003, Bush then invaded Iraq. Afghanistan became a strategic afterthought, with inadequate forces provided by the coalition. No concerted effort was made to train the disorganized Afghan army, let alone reform the police. Given aid and shelter inside treacherous Pakistan, the Taliban had regenerated their networks by 2005 and were attacking. In the southeast, the British Army set up outposts, some only single houses manned by a dozen soldiers. The Taliban would gather a force, shoot for several hours, then disperse. In the northeast, the Taliban trekked down the valleys from Pakistan, harassed isolated US Army outposts, then retreated across the border.

When I visited the country in mid-2006, senior officers were expressing deep unease about the besieged outpost strategy. General David McKiernan, commanding the coalition, pointed directly at Pakistan. "It all goes back to the problem set that there are sanctuaries," he said. "Insurgent groups are able to operate with impunity." Focused on Iraq, the Bush policymakers allowed the situation in Afghanistan to deteriorate.

When Barack Obama became president in 2009, he declared that "Afghanistan was the war that had to be won." Secretary of Defense Robert Gates followed up by confidently saying, "The United States really has gotten its head into this conflict only in the last year. We have a new policy set by our new president. We have a new strategy, a new mission…new military leadership also is needed." Gates dispatched his personal favorite, General Stanley McChrystal, to take command to implement the "new mission" of counterinsurgency.

That caught my attention. Having been on the ground for five years in Vietnam and having embedded frequently over six years in Iraq, I decided to embed with the frontline platoons to see how counterinsurgency was working in my third war. I was approaching seventy. I ran five miles daily, and to save weight on patrols, I wore fake cardboard armor and my Red Sox cap. The grunts didn't care if their grandfather traipsed along, as long as I didn't slow them up. I turned down offers to carry a weapon—too much weight—explaining there would be plenty around if needed.

In 2009, I embedded in the center of the fighting in the Korengal Valley in northeastern Kunar Province. This was hard-core Pashtun territory. Of the country's thirty million tribesmen, the Hazara tribe was dominant four hundred miles away in the west, and the Tajik tribe held the center-north seventy miles away. The ten million-strong Pashtun tribe, home to the Taliban movement, controlled the east along the 1,500-mile border with Pakistan.

Here in a jagged mountain range near Pakistan, the two thousand tribesmen in the Korengal were the most war-prone and insular. As I flew in, I snapped a picture of the valley. On the western hillside (to the right in the photo), the US Army had set up a company-sized (130 soldiers) outpost.

Korengal Valley: a death trap.

The tactical challenge was chilling. Clearing the steep hills on both sides was key to controlling the valley floor. In the best of weather, hiking up to the ridgelines took an exhausting day. Add in sniper fire, plus the need to send out patrols daily on both sides of the valley, and the mission seemed to me as a grunt well-nigh impossible. A week before I arrived, the soldiers of Viper Company, with whom I was embedding, had ambushed and killed fifteen armed Korengalis, a praiseworthy feat of arms. It was marred when the intrepid *New York Times* reporter Chris Chivers discovered that local Afghan soldiers had been selling their ammunition to the dead locals.

The villagers mourned and buried their relatives, then immediately struck back. On my first afternoon at Viper Company's outpost, I attended the memorial service for Pfc. Richard Dewater, twenty-one, killed on patrol the previous day. Rudyard Kipling had written about British soldiers who, after several years in school, had joined the army and ventured into tribal valleys like the Korengal. In *The Arithmetic of the Frontier*, he wrote:

> A great and glorious thing it is
> To learn, for seven years or so,
> The Lord knows what of that and this,
> Ere reckoned fit to face the foe—
> The flying bullet down the Pass,
> That whistles clear: "All flesh is grass."

A century after Kipling, the arithmetic of the frontier hadn't changed.

When the memorial service had ended, a dozen village elders with walking sticks hobbled through the barbed-wire gate to receive their weekly ration of aspirin and blood pressure pills. McChrystal wanted aid dispersed to every village. Treated well, the general believed, a tribal elder might prevent the next attack. Captain Jimmy Howell, the company commander, accepted the general's directive with professional equanimity.

"We give them medicine," he said, "and we don't get hit until they leave."

Sure enough, twenty minutes later, Russian 30-mm shells were peppering the ground around us. Howell responded by calling in mortars against rocky outcroppings seven hundred meters away. He had logged 990 fire missions in nine months. Patrols went out constantly, with the Korengalis deciding when to initiate contact.

Howell offered to show me the enemy. We trekked downslope to a stout cedar mosque, adjacent to a few dozen stone houses perched on stilts on the steep hillside. Local fighters were buried in the cemetery next to the mosque. In a *kahol* or extended family, if one son joined the Taliban, chances were high that several relatives would join the same gang. In the Korengal, they were interred side by side.

Outside the mosque, the *askars* (Afghan soldiers) accompanying us stacked their weapons and went inside to pray. In the culture of Afghanistan, adherence to Islam transcended the war. After the service, several dozen men and boys filed out and silently stared at us, dispassionate and unsmiling. Several had the beards favored by hardened Taliban fighters.

Korengalis: Willing to fight forever.

"You're looking at the guys we're fighting," Howell said. "It's weird out here. Our vehicles get blown up if we use the road in the valley. We're supplied by parachute. We race these guys to the drop zone. They usually snatch a few packets. Can't plug them for that. Besides, when they're stealing, they're not shooting at us."

Sharing the outpost with Viper Company were a hundred Afghan soldiers *(askars)* advised by Captain John Farris and seven Marines. Farris invited me to join his patrol, which was going to a hillside hamlet called Donna. As we lined up in combat formation, the Afghan interpreter, Mike, whispered to me.

"Captain John is really in charge," he said. "The askars don't respect their sergeants, and the Afghan sergeants don't respect their officers. They're all scared of the Taliban. They won't patrol without Captain John and his Marines."

Sucking wind at 7,400 feet altitude, we clambered up a rocky trail to reach a hamlet of a few dozen stone houses, with cows and goats munching hay on the balconies they shared with the humans. No children came out to gawk at us or beg for pens. Amid the crowing of the roosters, there were no murmurs of voices. The soldiers dispersed into nooks to avoid snipers, while Farris sat down behind a stone wall and lit a cigarette.

Farris had long ago given up winning hearts and minds. Occasionally he glanced at his map, with dozens of small crosses indicating artillery registration points. He had shown me an email that he had sent to his higher headquarters. "We conduct our KLEs [Key Leader Engagements] by going into villages to talk to the elders," he had written. "We sit there until all hell breaks loose, an effective if dangerous and uncreative way to locate the enemy."

Eventually, two elders, one with few teeth and the other with a short beard and a glum expression, wandered down and squatted next to him. No greetings, no smiles, no offering of chai. Farris languidly blew smoke. The elders knew he was waiting to get shot at, so that he could shoot back. Ten minutes passed in a silent Kabuki dance.

"We give stuff to these elders," Farris said to me. "Sometimes they take it, and sometimes they burn it. We offered to build a road. The villagers petitioned Abdul Rahman, a Taliban honcho in Pakistan. He said no. That ended the road."

The laughter of children carried up to the hamlet.

"The muj won't come out to play today," Farris continued. "They don't shoot around their own kids. We can pack it in."

Several months later, all US soldiers were pulled out of the Korengal. After six years of frustration and forty-two American lives lost, the high command decided to leave the valley. CNN ran a video showing Taliban soldiers pawing through the junk left behind in Howell's op center. Soon, all the other remote outposts in the northeast were also abandoned.

"American soldiers were an irritant to the people," General McChrystal, the top commander, explained. "There was probably much more fighting than there would have been [if US troops had never come]." It was a bewildering admission by the commander of our forces. If you don't intend to fight, don't invade another country.

Our soldiers pulled back to the flatlands a dozen miles to the west of the mountain range leading into Pakistan, where, in early 2009, I joined Battalion 1-32 of the Tenth Infantry Division. The mission of the seven hundred soldiers was to protect thirty thousand farmers spread across sixty villages. To protect them required finding and engaging the Taliban who lived in some villages, while others trekked back and forth from Pakistan. To do this, a US patrol mounted in Humvees visited each village once or twice a week, drinking tea with the elders and paying them a few hundred dollars for rarely completed projects. The villagers didn't report seeing any *dushmen* (bandits) or Taliban.

Major Jason Dempsey, the battalion's operations officer, showed me a picture of teenagers piling rocks on a path behind a US armored vehicle so that it could be ambushed. Minutes before, the boys had been waving at the soldiers.

"We Americans have been in Kunar Province for seven years," Dempsey said. "We haven't broken through with the people. And I don't know what to make of the government officials. They all cover their tracks. Some are crooks and others are straight."

As in Vietnam and Iraq, the insurgents hid as civilians among their fellow Pashtuns. The Afghan soldiers were mostly Tajiks, a traditional foe of the Pashtuns. The local Pashtun police drove around in shiny Toyota Hiluxes with no bullet holes. Live and let live. Every stone farmhouse was its own fortress. If a farmer wanted to stay out of the fight, as most did, that was all right. He knew or suspected which men in other compounds were insurgents. He was left alone, as long as he kept his mouth shut.

The chief bomb maker in the battalion's area was named Ajimal. After months of detective work, an informer pointed him out in a crowded market. To draw suspicion away from the informer, an Army platoon randomly apprehended a dozen male shoppers, including Ajimal. I watched as Ajimal laughed—as if he didn't have a care in the world. He casually slipped his cell phone to the next man in line, who slid it to the next, and so on. A boy at the edge of the crowd darted forward, took the phone, and edged away. US soldiers grabbed the phone and arrested Ajimal. The crowd had instinctively shielded him. His phone showed numerous calls to a Taliban cell in Pakistan. He was imprisoned and soon released. He immediately moved to Pakistan.

Battalion 1-32's base was only seven miles from Pakistan, and the frequent cross-border attacks vexed Lieutenant Colonel Fred O'Donnell, the battalion commander. The clandestine Taliban HF radio broadcasting from the mountains called him "that Christian invader." I accompanied him on an arduous climb to the 9,500-foot border. When he arrived unannounced at a Pakistan outpost, the startled border guards pointed at a castle-like compound several hundred yards downslope on the Pakistan side. From there, they admitted, *dushmen* led donkeys carrying arms into Afghanistan. Their instruction was not to interfere in "Afghan matters."

On the battalion base two nights later, I was awakened by a shuddering car-umph. Rockets had hit the munitions bunker, igniting spectacular orange and red explosions. Fortunately, the only injury was the battalion's pride.

The following day, I joined a platoon going into Dangam district on the very edge of the Pakistan border. The leader, Lieutenant Jake Kerr, was a rugged rugby player admired by his troops, genial with the people and zestful in firefights. On the single dirt road leading to the border, the platoon found and detonated two IEDs. Arriving at the district headquarters, Kerr saw that the fortifications his platoon had laboriously built were sagging in disrepair. The police offered us flatbread, provided we pay five dollars per loaf.

"I spent months doing all this work for you," Kerr snapped, "and this is how you treat us?"

The oleaginous district chief shrugged; all was peaceful. He did, though, pass on a message. The Taliban leader, Zamar, challenged Kerr to cross the border and meet with him. That afternoon, through binoculars, we picked out three Taliban watching us from a cliff.

The next day, we walked back in the steaming heat of the approaching summer months. To refresh myself, I broke open a watermelon and savored its sugary juice. A few hours later, I flew north with the battalion. The mission was to protect an obscure town called Barge Matal. Halfway there, we landed to refuel. By then, my head was splitting and my insides were burning. I staggered to a ditch where everything inside me gushed out of every opening. A squad leader, Sergeant Eric Lindstrom, carried me to the aid station. He packed my rucksack and set it beside me, telling me to get well. As I lay on a stretcher, the doctor peered at me, promising, "You're not going to die on me." I kept vomiting and shitting, and he kept pumping fluids into me. When I wobbled on board a medevac chopper to Bagram Air Base, the crew chief asked me to step into a plastic bag, then put another one over my head, with openings for me to vomit and shit into a huge barrel.

"Trying to keep my bird clean," he said.

For two days, I lay in an isolated ward, with three IVs dripping into me. The watermelon I had eaten had been grown in shit water, and I was down with mountain cholera. On the third day, Lieutenant Jake Miraldi was carried in. I had been on a patrol with him when a few of his troops had fallen back. He had stopped and waited, not reprimanding his exhausted soldiers—a thoughtful leader. Hit in the leg by an RPG, Jake was dripping blood. The doctor had closed his wounds with staples. I kidded him not to mess up my clean ward.

"I lost Eric Lindstrom," Jake said. "He was kneeling next to me when the rocket hit. He took most of it."

In my pack were my Oakley sunglasses, packed tightly by Eric to prevent breakage. Jake said that was typical; Eric had looked out for everyone in his squad.

The purpose of the mission to Barge Matal was to allow the residents to vote in the presidential election. Jake estimated he had collected about three hundred ballots. Karzai won the election, including over a thousand votes from Barge Matal. While the battalion was in Barge Matal, the Taliban seized Dangam district, which I had just visited with Lt. Jake Kerr.

I flew back to the States, taking several months to recover. When I rejoined Battalion 1-32 in the fall of 2009, they had just finished another battle. The Afghan soldiers had scheduled a friendship visit to Ganjigal, a small village on a plateau leading into Pakistan. Forewarned, scores of Taliban had set up machine guns and hammered the unsuspecting friendly force. I described the battle in the book, *Into the Fire,* coauthored with Corporal Dakota Meyer, who fought valiantly there.

Fifteen Afghan soldiers were killed in Ganjigal. No firepower had been directed at Ganjigal before or during the battle. The villagers harbored no resentment over past deeds or misunderstandings. The Afghan troops had even brought copies of the Quran to distribute as tokens of friendship. Yet not one villager said a word as the Afghan troops walked past them into the waiting ambush. Five American advisors and eight askar Afghan soldiers were killed inside the hamlet.

General McChrystal insisted that "the conflict will be won by persuading the population, not by destroying the enemy." The deceit at Ganjigal demonstrated the limits of that benevolent counterinsurgency theory. In South Vietnam, the villagers did welcome soldiers like Corporal Phil Brannon into their hamlets. In Iraq, the Sunni tribes had come over to the side of America, the strongest tribe. In Afghanistan, the Pashtun tribes adhered to a culture and to tenets of Islam that tied them closer to the Taliban than to the government in Kabul and the foreigners fighting for that government.

* * *

In mid-2009, McChrystal shifted the counterinsurgency effort from the isolated hamlets in the northeast to the flat farming villages of the southeast, where drugs provided the finances for the Taliban. Twenty-five thousand US Marines were deployed to take control of Helmand Province, the opium capital of the world. The province was mostly desert, bisected by the Helmand River, which ran north to south for seven hundred miles, providing copious water for a narrow fertile valley called the Green Zone. Rich in corn, wheat, and especially poppy, the Green Zone was enclosed by tree lines and dense undergrowth, interlaced with thousands of irrigation ditches.

The intent was for US troops to clear the two thousand villages of the Taliban, then turn them over to Afghan forces to hold and to build dispensaries, schools, roads, and the like, thus, by material favors, cementing the loyalty of the villages to the government in Kabul. US forces would clear villages and Afghan soldiers would hold them, like an ever-expanding ink blot.

In June 2009, I embedded with a battalion (six hundred Marines) in Nawa district. When I arrived, no shops were open and the market was deserted. Daily rations for the Marines consisted of bottles of warm water and two MREs (Meals Ready to Eat) in plastic bags. There were no refrigerators, no air conditioning, and no escape from the dust and the smothering one-hundred-degree heat. A schoolhouse next to the battalion headquarters housed sixty askars, advised by six British soldiers.

The first afternoon, I joined a squad patrol. We walked across open fields, with the sun behind us and no wind. Perfect sniper conditions. The first shots came from the west, cracking high. To outflank the shooter, Sergeant Robert Kightlinger vaulted over a compound wall and into a stinking creek used as a latrine by the farmers. I followed with a few Marines as more rounds clipped overhead. A heavy caliber round smacked into the wall above our heads, splattering stone chips around us. "There!" Kightlinger shouted, pointing to a puff of dust from a farmhouse four hundred meters away. His adrenaline pumping, he weighed the risk of moving by bounds across an open field the size of a football field. *Wham!* Another heavy round knocked a chip of concrete off the wall.

"Bravo 2, you're too exposed," Lieutenant Shawn Connor, the platoon commander, radioed. "Get back here."

In the falling light, we waded chest-high through the shit water and returned to the platoon. The Taliban said goodbye by throwing a few taunting shots after us.

"Damn, Kightlinger," Connor said, "you stink."

Kightlinger sucked in a lungful of air and shook his head. "Hard to finish a fight, sir," he said.

The battalion commander, Lieutenant Colonel Bill McCollough, wasn't going to play this whack-a-mole. He organized a complete clean-up. Broken down into thirty squads, the entire battalion set out to sweep, day and night, across the fields and through the tree lines, searching every compound. In one giant, continuous, unceasing movement, the district was to be cleared from end to end.

For the sweep, British Captain Edward Brown invited me to join his five advisors, called Amber 4, and fifty askars. Before pushing off, he coordinated his sector with those of the Marine battalion. Few film scenes provided a better send-up of a Hollywood war movie than watching Brown—badly in need of a haircut, his slender runner's body clad in only sandals and spandex shorts, pointer in hand at a map—addressing the heavily muscled Marines. Despite having served on battlefields in four countries, he looked absurdly young.

"Right, mates," Brown began in an upper-class accent that clipped each syllable. "My job is to start from the western canal and push the tangos [Taliban] into your waiting arms. My askars look like Afghans, because that's what they are. Nobody shoot to the west, please. Your bullets tend to hurt, and that will demoralize my askars."

When the sweep kicked off, Brown, who had run cross-country at Sandhurst, set a torrid pace. Inside two hundred yards, we were passing the lead Marines who were carrying much heavier loads. We smiled as we walked by prepossessing Sergeant Bill Cahir, an older reservist who had volunteered for the frontlines. Worn down by his pack, he rented a donkey for sixty dollars to carry his load. Good plan; poor execution. The donkey bucked off Cahir's gear and refused to move.

Sergeant Bill Cahir with the stubborn donkey.

We pushed ahead. Shortly later, the point scouts bumped straight into two tangos surprised by Brown's speed. After mutually wild shooting and yelling, the Talibs ran away unscathed.

"Twenty bloody feet away from the bastards," bemoaned Cpl. Ben Woodhouse, the point man, "and I missed!"

For the next four days, there were a few incoming rounds from snipers each dawn, then a desultory search of several compounds before both sides settled into the shade of separate farms. By ten in the morning, it was too hot to move, let alone to fight. On the fifth day, Private Matt Levers saw a man peering from a nearby farm wall called "dickers" for obvious reasons. Levers snapped off a shot that startled a Talib machine gunner about 150 meters away. He promptly opened fire. With heavy PKM slugs cracking over our heads, we crawled to an outhouse where the shit fell into a ditch. We slipped into that stinking water to emerge on the Talibs' flank.

Assuming the Taliban had pulled back, I scrambled out of the undergrowth to adjust my camera. The Brits screamed at me, frantically pointing at a nearby tree line. I didn't see the shooter but there was no mistaking the sharp *bang!* of a rocket-propelled grenade launcher. Before I could move, the rocket hit the branch above my head. Leaves fluttered down around me as it spun away before harmlessly detonating. A sure kill shot spoiled by a branch.

A kill shot spoiled by a branch.

By week's end, the Marines had scoured the district, losing no one while killing only a few. McCollough then dispersed his squads into twenty-five interlaced outposts, each responsible for security in two of the district's fifty villages. To my surprise, he named eight outposts after the fallen Marines described in my book *The Village*: Sullivan, Brannon, Foster, and the others. McCollough's orders were simple: Treat the farmers with respect and shoot the Taliban. He offered to pay the farmers to form a militia, as we had done in Vietnam. The offer was politely but firmly declined. The district was populated by the Barakzai tribe that, while resentful of the Taliban, didn't want to be accused of helping infidels who would leave sooner or later. Every day the Marines conducted over a hundred patrols. No farmer went into his fields without bumping into a patrol. The poppy fields were left untouched. So as not to antagonize the farmers, the grunts walked carefully among the fresh green plants.

One farmer asked the Marines to stand guard while he moved his stash of wet opium. The elders in another village asked the Marines not to patrol on a certain day so that a buyer from Balochistan could appraise their poppy crop.

Poppy everywhere.

One day I hitched a ride to an outpost with three askars in a Ford Ranger pickup truck. On an open stretch of road, the driver suddenly stopped. For a moment I feared I had made a fatal mistake. Instead, an askar furtively hopped out, and in seconds, scrambled back in, cradling a watermelon. Concerned I might report them, they offered me a slice. I firmly refused. I didn't explain why I hated watermelon.

With American patrols ubiquitous, the Taliban pulled out of the district but kept probing along the outskirts. I spent a few days with twenty Marines at an outpost harassed by constant sniping. Exasperated one afternoon by shots from a scrubby pine grove not two hundred meters away, Connor sent out Kightlinger and two grunts. I tagged along. Amid the sparse pines, we spotted two Talibs sprinting to a one-room shack with mud-caked walls. Kightlinger radioed back that he was moving forward to pitch in grenades.

"Negative," Connor called back. "I'm not trading your ass for that of a five-dollar-a-day Taliban."

In platoons north and south, I saw this moral balancing act time and again: What comes first, carrying out a frustrating mission or protecting your men?

Nawa became the showcase for counterinsurgency. The shops were again selling clothes, shovels, propane, and vegetables. The Americans and Brits bargained with the merchants for fresh vegetables. Helmets and armor weren't worn in the bazaar. On Fridays, the market was packed with more than a thousand farmers buying and selling sheep, cows, and camels. McCollough established a district council, opened schools, appointed a police chief, and paid workers to clean out the weed-infested irrigation canals. Congressmen from the States and four-star generals flocked to the district. President Karzai and McChrystal visited. The Chairman of the Joint Chiefs of Staff said, "This is an example of what we expect the results of the surge [of additional US troops] to be."

By 2010, Nawa was definitely a success. The smiling, rotund district chief Haji Abdul Manaf (later assassinated) called McCollough "the real district chief." That was both the near-term truth and the long-term mortal flaw; eventually, the Americans would leave.

With Nawa bustling, McCollough sent his units farther afield. I joined Cahir, who had rented the balking donkey, on a four-mile hike to a hamlet that had never seen an American soldier. It was so remote that Alexander the Great may have passed it by. A hundred bewildered locals turned out to gawk at us. A plump mullah dressed in black was looking quizzically at my wrinkled face. He pointed at my Red Sox cap with its red B. Through Sam, our interpreter, I explained the Sox were the world's baseball champions. Oh. Did I play for them? The Marines grinned when I answered with a bit of exaggeration.

"How many hits did you get?" the mullah asked.

"One or two a game," I modestly replied.

The mullah murmured, and the crowd burst out laughing.

"I told them baseball is like cricket," Sam sheepishly explained. "The mullah says you're the worst batsman in the world. That's why, in your old age, your team banished you here."

Grinning, Cahir thanked me for loosening up the crowd and launched into his pitch that we had come in peace. A few weeks later, affable Sgt. Bill Cahir was shot in the neck and killed.

* * *

In the winter of 2011, I returned to southern Helmand Province just as a drug-clearing operation was kicking off. Twice a year, when the purple and white poppy flowers blossomed, workers cut a tiny nick in each bulb. The sap flowed out, with the sun searing it black. Paid ten dollars a day, the workers sliced off each black teardrop. An acre of teardrops added up to ten pounds of wet poppy, with chemicals boiling that down to a kilo of pure heroin. The field workers, often part-time Taliban, earned $2,000 each. The lab workers boiling the poppy netted $5,000, while the farmer took in $15,000, five times the profit from wheat or corn. Afghanistan was providing 90 percent of the world's heroin, bringing in a billion dollars a year, with Taliban, Iranian, Pakistani, and Afghan officials taking their cuts.

In February, thousands of Marines stormed into the Marjah district, a heroin hub. For the assault, I joined Army Special Forces Team 3121, a dozen soldiers whose average age was over thirty, most on their third tour. They were advising an Afghan battalion whose leaders were hiding in the rear. In their absence, Captain Matt Golsteyn, on his third tour, became the de facto commander. What he ordered, two hundred askars carried out, staying behind their Special Forces advisors.

Matt had "liberated" a massive four-story concrete edifice with five skylights, dubbed Thunder Dome after a James Bond movie. Its owner was a drug lord who had fled to Kabul. On the roof one afternoon, Matt (in black cap) saw through binoculars five tangos eight hundred meters away, out of rifle range. The mustachioed air controller (Captain Justin "Woody" Woodruff, a Marine captain) radioed for a Cobra strike.

Captain Matt Golsteyn (l) and Captain Justin Woodruff.

The Cobra slid forward, emitting what sounded like a long burp as billows of dust from 30-mm shells swept up the road. One Talib fell, and the others scrambled inside the compound, which was off-limits because a family might be inside.

"They've reached home plate, guys," Woody said. "They're safe. That wraps it up."

That's how most operations proceeded: brief flurries that slowly pushed back the Taliban. On the fourth day, Matt sent a team to clear the buildings in a local square. A few hours later, we heard a sharp boom. We rushed to the square, now a shambles of twisted metal, smashed-in doors, and strewn trash. Two Marine engineers, assigned to help the Special Forces, had opened a garage door and been blown to bits.

To find the bomb maker, Matt's team employed all its clandestine sources and methods. The following week, a farmer agreed to point out the bomb maker. Matt brought both of them to the district police. To his astonishment, the police chief let the bomb maker go, who walked out cursing and promising to kill the farmer. Matt followed the bomb maker, who was never seen again.

(I had recommended Matt to the CIA's Special Operations branch. Back in the States in 2012, Matt took a CIA polygraph and allegedly said he had executed the bomb maker to protect the informant. The Army charged him with murder but had no witnesses. Nonetheless, the Army found him guilty of conduct unbecoming an officer, revoked his medals for valor, and dismissed him from the service. In 2019, President Donald Trump pardoned Matt.)

* * *

Within two weeks, Marjah seemed under control, and Afghan officials arrived to manage the district. This was described by McChrystal as "government in a box." President Barack Obama flew to Afghanistan, where he said, "Our troops have pushed the Taliban out of their stronghold in Marjah."

In response, the Taliban avoided the Americans and launched a murder and intimidation campaign against the locals. Soon, stories abounded of night letters and beatings. Eight elders were beheaded. Finding dollar bills in the pocket of an eight-year-old boy, the Talibs hanged him. Throughout Marjah, there were one-room mosques with loudspeakers on flat roofs. Anti-government invective echoed daily through the fields. Like an itinerant preacher in nineteenth-century America, a mullah made a living based on oratorical skills and connecting with the farmers. For a mullah to preach radical Islam both protected him from assassination and guaranteed a livelihood.

"Killing the enemy," General McChrystal believed, "was not the best route to success. It's really about convincing the people that they want it [the Taliban insurgency] to stop and they ultimately will."[2] When McChrystal visited Marjah, he asked the district governor whether he liked the bakery in the market. The governor said he never ventured into the market. In a testy mood, McChrystal took the Marine commander aside, telling him he didn't have all the time in the world to get the job done.

"I can give you a slow win, General," Lieutenant Colonel Brian Christmas said, "or a fast defeat. A fast win isn't possible. The people won't cooperate."

The general left, and the grunts continued to patrol constantly. But unlike in Nawa, the sniper fire didn't cease. To avoid being hit, the troops slept in the dirt, as though in graves.

Living the dream, Marine-style.

It was rough and grimy, made more so because there was no breakthrough with the farmers who wanted the Americans to leave.

* * *

I moved on from Marjah to Now Zad, one hundred kilometers to the north. It looked like a tornado had passed through the town, ripping up houses and strewing debris on every street. Only six thousand of the twenty thousand residents had moved back since the Marines had pushed out the Taliban. Captain Jason Brezler, tall and raw-boned, offered to show me what was going on. In civilian life, Jason served in the New York City Fire Department.

"I took a year's leave to do this tour," he said. "Now I have my own city. Needs a little repair, but we'll get there."

After dark, we moved down the backstreets through the mud and sleet. Jason rapped softly on an iron gate, a door creaked open, and we walked downstairs into a tiny cellar heated by a small wood stove. A half dozen townsmen smiled as we pulled off our stinking boots and sank into cushions around the walls. Our host, Sardar Mohamed, offered slices of tomatoes and flatbread before tugging out a harmonica-accordion, a 1930s contraption that groaned out a musical tune. The Afghans boisterously clapped and bonged songs. Sardar had risked his life to hide the harmonica during years under Taliban rule. It was a bizarre setting in a cellar lit by candles in a bombed-out city.

"How're things?" Jason asked.

"Excellent," Sardar said. "You *samandari* are good government."

"Sardar, we're not your government. We're Americans and we're leaving."

"No, you cannot! The Taliban gave our land deeds to the Ishaqzai tribe," Sardar said. "We Barakzais are accused of giving up Islam because we talk with you infidels."

"Sardar, I can't judge land deeds," Jason said. "Ask your own government, or the mullahs."

"The mullahs can be bought," Sardar said. "You are our government."

There it was, the pattern of choosing sides that I saw time and again. The hundreds of Pashtun subtribes in eastern Afghanistan had divided into two cliques. The larger group was hostile and aligned with the Taliban, as in the Korengal and Marjah. A smaller group, as in Nawa and Now Zad, was receptive to the Americans among them. But that group had no solid links to the government. Worse still, on the other side of the moon back in Kabul, President Karzai routinely railed against stationing US or allied troops in the villages, complaining that it upset the traditional rural governing structure—that did not exist.

* * *

In mid-2010, General David Petraeus replaced General Stanley McChrystal as the top commander. Petraeus's guidance to the 140,000 coalition troops was to persist in counterinsurgency. The problems, however, were insurmountable. The number of villages vastly outnumbered the number of coalition platoons. In Helmand Province alone, there were two thousand villages and hamlets. The Marines could deploy 240 squads. One squad per ten villages was impossible odds. There were not anywhere near the number of troops required. More constraining still, the Afghan Islamic culture prevented any real interaction between foreign male unbelievers and family members. Unlike in Vietnam, in Afghanistan (and Iraq) there were no Combined Action Platoons where a dozen Marines lived among several thousand villagers. There were no Binh Nghias.

It was the same story in the north, where Army Battalion 1-32 was returning to the States. I flew up to say goodbye. Lt. Jake Miraldi had recovered from his wounds and was again leading his platoon.

"In my zone, I visit seventeen villages at least once every two weeks," he said. "One visit for a few hours to a village every week or two—how much difference do we make?"

Company commander Capt. Mike Harrison, wrapping up his second tour, had spent endless hours sipping tea, supervising projects, and supporting local officials.

"Some people are on our side, and some aren't," Harrison said. "We haven't broken the shadow government of the Taliban. Everyone likes our money, but that hasn't changed their attitudes."

At the close of 2010, I could not reconcile what the policymakers and generals were saying with what I saw on the ground. I had spent six years in the field in Vietnam, five years of embeds in Iraq, and four years in Afghanistan. In my book, *The Wrong War*, I explained why counterinsurgency could not succeed.

Petraeus's counterinsurgency guidance to the troops was to "secure and serve the population" because "the people were the center of gravity." I cited examples across many provinces where it was arithmetically impossible to "secure" the villagers; there simply weren't enough coalition troops. Obama had acknowledged that his strategy

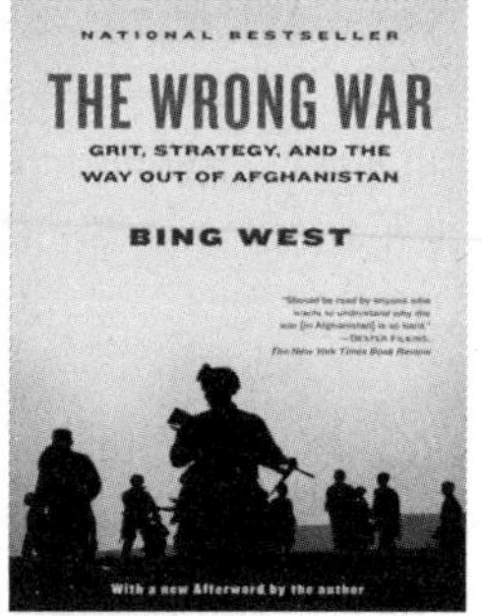

An impulsive war, fought the wrong way.

was "not fully resourced counterinsurgency." Without the resources, the effort was at best a gesture. The Afghan soldiers weren't holding the countryside. Pakistan was providing the Taliban with an impregnable sanctuary. The Taliban were woven into the Islamic fabric of the Pashtun tribal society, while the Afghan government failed to foster a spirit of nationalism.

For ten years, our troops had done the work of others. I advocated pulling out our conventional combat forces, ceasing with the counterinsurgency mission, and bulking up our special forces and advisors to train the Afghan army. "Killing the enemy," McChrystal said, "was not the best route to success. It's really about convincing the people that they want it [the insurgency by the Taliban] to stop and they ultimately will."[3] That was crazy talk. The people were not the center of gravity; they were the prize. The center of gravity was creating an Afghan force that could beat the Taliban in battle. *The New York Times* placed *The Wrong War* on the cover of its Sunday book review section. While it was a bestseller, the Pentagon refused to comment on what I had written. Counterinsurgency persisted as the core mission.

* * *

In 2011 to 2012, I again embedded in Helmand Province, where more Americans had died than anywhere else. I checked in with Colonel Paul Kennedy, whom I knew from the 2004 battle for Ramadi in Iraq. One of his units—Battalion 3/5—was assigned to a district called "Bloody Sangin" by the Brits, who were forced to pull out. In their first month, 3/5 suffered fifteen dead, forty amputations, and seventy others wounded. Lieutenant Robert Kelly was among those killed. After his funeral, the press circulated the remarks of his father, Marine three-star Lieutenant General John Kelly: "We always hope for friendship…. But if it's death they want, it's death they will get."

There was no talk about winning hearts and minds in Sangin. It was a straight-up slugfest. Twenty percent of the battalion was put out of action in the opening weeks of a seven-month deployment. Secretary of Defense Robert Gates agonized about pulling out the battalion. Kennedy and the commandant of the Marine Corps persuaded him not to do so, arguing that Marines don't quit.

"You want to know what's going on?" Kennedy said to me. "I have the platoon for you. I'll take you there."

After driving thirty kilometers, we stopped on a dirt road in the middle of farming country. In the spring of 2011, on both sides of us sprouted the tall corn and shorter poppy fields of the Green Zone. Waiting was Lieutenant Vic Garcia, a wrestling champion in high school who looked like he spent his spare time lifting Humvees. Kennedy wished me luck and drove off.

"My platoon's a mile inside the Green Zone," Vic said. "No vehicle can get there."

Six of us walked, or zigzagged, west. Breathing was tough whenever we cut inside the rows of corn, where the moist air was sucked up by the burning sun. At one point, a small green cobra slithered across our path. When we emerged into the stubby poppy fields, the grunts spread widely apart, wary of snipers in the tree lines that marked the shallow canals leading to the Helmand River. The fort holding Vic's fifty-two Marines was a run-down farm encircled in barbed wire, with one watch tower.

Inside the patrol base, eponymously named "Fires," a well provided a trickle of water to wring out sweat-soaked clothes. Sleeping quarters were caves hacked out of the crumbling walls. For dinner, the squads heated their plastic-wrapped food over a few open fires, fueled by tree branches. Barbequed goat was a luxury. There were no cell phones, no internet, no link to home or to the outside world.

On daily patrols, the grunts talked only briefly to petulant farmers who asked for money. Families of all ages tilled the fields, ignoring the Marines passing by. When the people fled, it signaled

Lieutenant Vic Garcia (with shaved head) and author at Patrol Base Fires.

that Taliban nearby were preparing to shoot. On one patrol, when we walked by a courtyard where a mullah was instructing a dozen boys, the air was thick with silent hostility. Such tiny mosques were everywhere, producing recruits for the Taliban. Whatever fueled the mystique of the Taliban—be it Islamic fervor, or the excitement of belonging to a holy warrior caste—it was real. The Taliban imposed moderate taxes, permitted the flow of electricity from a hydroelectric dam, and ran a shadow government, complete with judges.

A few askars did walk in trace near the tail end of each patrol, but it was the Marines' fight. Outside the wire, the grunts moved so slowly and quietly that we once scared three slumbering coyotes, who tore away, yipping. Each day brought a skirmish. Every grunt's rifle held a telescopic sight, and the Talibs had learned to shoot only from long range. The occasional flurry of incoming bullets was the same I had experienced in many other places. We'd flop down and return fire. Nothing out of the ordinary about the brief exchanges of bullets.

The difference was the sheer quantity of the IEDs. Each patrol wended its way single file, with no grunt stepping outside the dabs of shaving cream squirted by the point man. On my first day, Lance Corporal Colbey Yazzie, the unflappable engineer in the lead with the metal detector, uncovered three IEDs and playfully threw one—disabled—to me. It consisted of two boards the length of a ruler, held apart by a sponge, with a wire soldered in the center. The wire was attached to a jug of explosives made from fertilizer and a battery buried several feet away. A foot stepping on the IED boards connected the wire to the battery, sending an electrical impulse to the explosives. These rigs, costing less than five dollars each, were buried randomly in the rich soil. Yazzie uncovered thirty-eight IEDs in seven months, only to lose his leg to the thirty-ninth IED.

The grunts did not shorten their patrols to reduce the danger from the IEDs. One patrol chased a Taliban gang for six hours in

Corporal Yazzie uncovers an IED.

a running gunfight. Some Marines attached tourniquets to their trousers before patrolling. Vic put a stop to that because it affected morale. His grunts called him "The Juggernaut."

Of the fifty-two grunts who deployed from the States, two were killed, nine lost limbs, and a dozen more took gunshot or shrapnel wounds. In seven months, half the platoon was killed or wounded. Etched into the hardened clay of the outpost's wall was a cross of Saint David, with forty-seven stick figures alongside.

"Ten of them," a sniper explained, "for each one of us. That's our goal."

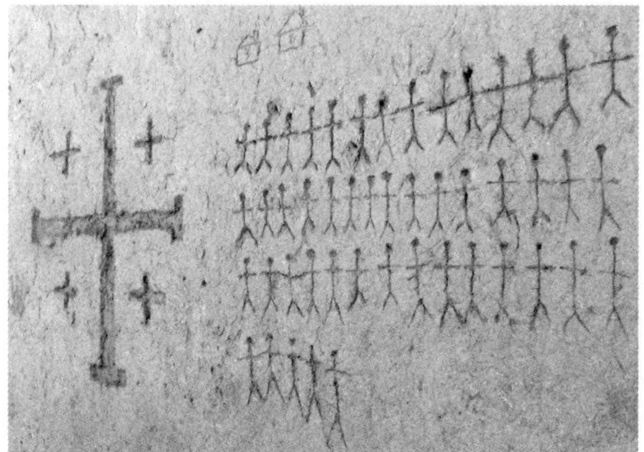

Kill count etched into the Sangin outpost wall.

In their last week in the country, one of the three squad leaders lost his foot to an IED. Over the course of the seven-month deployment, I calculated that every grunt in Vic's platoon had walked one million steps on patrol, risking legs, arms, testicles, and stomach. It seemed fitting to entitle my book, *One Million Steps: A Marine Platoon at War.*

The platoon knew their effort was for naught. None believed that Afghan soldiers

176 Brits and Marines died in Sangin, the bloodiest district in Afghanistan.

would venture into the Green Zone once they left. Sergeant Joe "Mad Dog" Myers, responsible for calling in the artillery, was Vic's shadow on patrols. When Vic wanted fire, he wanted it *right now.* Mad Dog entertained the platoon by imitating the sounds of the fires he called in. He held no illusions about progress.

"This war's stupid," he said to me. "Well, so what? Our country's in it."

Sergeant Joe Myers exhorting the troops.

Years after leaving Sangin, Mad Dog lost his battle with drug addiction. On the Amazon page of *One Million Steps,* a close friend of Mad Dog wrote, "Serving his country was his greatest honor."

I returned to Sangin in 2012. Battalion 1/7 (my old unit from Vietnam) faced the same tenacious Taliban and sullen tribes as had Vic Garcia. The mission had changed to training and putting the Afghan soldiers in the lead. On patrols, though, the askars still dawdled behind the Marines. Most of the askars were Tajiks from four hundred miles north. Few spoke Pashto, and conversations with the farmers were standoffish. Patrol routes had been shortened in length and duration. Once back at an outpost, the askars had to stack their weapons, watched by a Marine posted in a machine-gun tower. This injected distrust. But coalition soldiers had been killed on several bases by assassins dressed in Afghan uniforms.

After my book was published in 2015, the Marine three-star general in Afghanistan wrote to me, observing that I understood tactics but not operations or strategy. I wrote back, observing that his operation as the commander had failed because the enemy still held Sangin. As for the counterinsurgency strategy of persuading the farmers to oppose the Taliban, I wrote that in my embeds from 2006 through 2012, I had not seen one village militia successfully defending its own hamlets. Farmers weren't fighters. The Taliban had a religious fervor and ferocity in battle that the Afghan soldiers, disconnected from the dysfunctional Kabul government, lacked.

By 2017, the Taliban had seized Marjah, Now Zad, Nawa, and Sangin. The efforts and sacrifices of our grunts from the Korengal in the north to Sangin in the south had gone for naught. I sat down and spent three years writing *The Last Platoon,* published in 2020. It was a novel in which every character, from PFC to president, was a real person I had known. I described the nature of the twenty-year war by focusing on one last, seven-day operation in Helmand Province. My purpose was to contrast the reality of battle on the ground with the distorted policies at the top.

Afghanistan Policy: Why We Lost

The war in Afghanistan was lost due to seven mistakes.

Mistake 1: Letting Al Qaeda escape

In November 2001, Al Qaeda leader Osama bin Laden and his core fighters, battered by air strikes, had retreated into snow-bound mountains near the Pakistan border. To destroy them, the CIA urged President George W. Bush to employ the elite US task force that was standing by, primed to fight. Instead, Bush deferred to the theater commander in Tampa, FL, who gave the mission to Afghan warlords. They allowed Bin Laden and his force to escape into Pakistan. Secretary of Defense Donald Rumsfeld later told me the president chose not to intervene in the military chain of command. As commander in chief, Bush failed to make the key command decision.

Mistake 2: Committing to a multi-decade democracy

After Al Qaeda escaped, Bush changed the mission. He decided to shape Afghanistan into a Western democracy. Our military, intelligence, and diplomatic communities did not point out that a democracy would take decades to build. There was no strategy specifying the time horizon or resources required. A democracy could not be erected and solidified during his tenure, and no request was made for Congress to vote on such a weighty and long-term project.

Mistake 3: Tolerating the Pakistan sanctuary

Bush declared after 9/11 that nations were either "with us or against us." Yet he knew that treacherous Pakistan was sheltering both Al Qaeda and the Taliban leaders. "The primary cause of the trouble in Afghanistan," he said, "came from Pakistan."[1] Still, he tolerated the deceivers.

Was there an alternative? Pakistan was the sole land route to deliver the massive logistics needed for the American way of war. International aid provided the life support for Pakistan's mismanaged economy. Breaking Pakistan's economy would cause chaos in a nation that possessed both nuclear bombs and its own domestic terrorists. A less extreme step was to cut off most international funds and forsake using its land route. That meant the US would have to fight a different kind of war, with US regular units pared back and Special Forces restructuring the Afghan army to fight the Taliban.

After we abandoned Afghanistan in 2021, General Frank McKenzie, in charge of the Central Command, wrote that a decade earlier he had concluded, "Unless we were able to choke off this haven for them, we were doomed to failure."[2] Successive presidents and Chairmen of the Joint Chiefs of Staff chose to ignore intelligence warnings that Pakistan, supportive of Islamist causes and aligned with China, was not a friend.

Mistake 4: Nation-building as military malpractice

When President Barack Obama took office in 2009, he declared, "They [the Taliban] must be defeated."[3] At the same time, Chairman of the Joint Chiefs of Staff Admiral Michael Mullen and our generals were repeatedly saying, "We can't kill our way to victory."[4] That sentiment substituted compassion for logic. War is the premeditated, deliberate act of killing your enemies, until they are removed from power or agree to your terms. If you do not intend to kill, do not go to war.

In 2008, Secretary of Defense Robert Gates thoroughly confused both himself and the troops. "We cannot kill or capture our way to victory," he said. "Where possible, kinetic operations should be subordinate to measures to promote better governance, economic programs to spur development, and efforts to address grievances among the discontented."[5] Governance, development, and grievance resolution were diplomatic, not military missions. The Taliban believed they could kill their way to victory, and they did. With no hint that he grasped the irony, Gates later wrote, "Troops need to be told their goal is to defeat those trying to kill them."[6] The troops understood that; the policymakers, including Gates, did not.

General Stanley McChrystal was the top commander in 2009. "I was asking soldiers to believe," he later wrote, "in something their ground-level experience denied them."[7] That sentence summarized the futility of the generals' ordering our grunts to be nation-builders.

Mistake 5: Misunderstanding counterinsurgency

Counterinsurgency operations were supposed to seep ever outward, like an ink spot. American troops would clear the Taliban from village after village, then be replaced by motivated Afghan troops. This was doomed from the start. The "troop-to-task" ratio was impossible. There were only a thousand US/allied platoons to clear 10,000 villages. Even if that is done, as in Nawa district where Sgt. Cahir was killed, to train a local force to take requires more than a year, if ever. Even in Nawa, the askars refused to patrol once the Americans left, because the Taliban were fiercer fighters. Every successive US commanding general claimed there was progress. This was not true. The Pentagon never conducted a lessons-learned postmortem to determine whether senior officers were disingenuous, or whether our military system was, from top to bottom, driven by a "can-do" spirit of emphasizing the positive that rendered impossible cold, candid assessments from moving up the chain of command.

Our generals tried to duplicate their success in Iraq, without recognizing that the two wars were fundamentally different. The Sunni tribes in Iraq came over because they needed US protection from Al Qaeda and from the Shiite government. In Afghanistan, the opposite was true. The fierce Pashtun tribes, adhering to their Islamic traditions, provided the wellspring for the Taliban movement. No outside Al Qaeda-type terrorists threatened the tribes. It was never explained what "winning hearts and minds" meant in practical terms. Hearts and minds matter only if the tribes' resources and information are linked to a superior armed force. Otherwise, the side with the weapons rules, regardless of sympathies.

Our generals persisted too long in pursuing an unworkable counterinsurgency theory before shifting in 2013 to the training of the Afghan army. This waste of a decade wore down US domestic support for the war.

Mistake 6: Championing losers

Our policymakers refrained from choosing the indigenous leaders qualified to fill the senior echelons of command. This hands-off approach reflected the post-colonial philosophy that we do not impose our preferred leaders upon another country. As a consequence, we tolerated corrupt, ineffective officers and civilian officials at all levels. Familial and tribal patronage pervaded. From the Kabul capital down to the districts, positions depended on paying bribes upward and extorting payments downward.

In contrast, the Taliban promoted upward from the subtribes. When one leader was killed, another proven fighter took his place. The Talibs promoted from their ranks those who shared a blazing belief in their medieval Islamist cause.

The erratic President Hamid Karzai reigned for ten years, ranting against the American government while treating the Taliban with deference. His successor, Ashraf Ghani, antagonized both his political partners and tribal chieftains. Neither man instituted promotion based upon merit or imbued confidence in the security forces. When the Taliban seized control, a terrified Ghani fled the county. Karzai remained with the Taliban, living comfortably in his wealthy residence in Kabul. President Bush had tried to guide him, but he never believed in what Bush was selling. Our policymakers championed senior Afghan officials who were losers.

Mistake 7: Quitting

A full Taliban victory was not inevitable. From 2013 onward, the focus changed to training the Afghan army. The askars had no faith in their own chain of command; they did trust our advisors and air power. Battlefield tactics shifted to what the Afghan army could do: play defense. Afghan soldiers, not Americans or allies, did the fighting and dying.

In 2017, the Kabul government controlled the cities and the country's interior, while the Taliban ruled the rural eastern districts adjacent to Pakistan. The US was employing overhead surveillance, spies, and bombing to encourage the Afghan army to hold the line. In 2013, there were 2,400 air strikes; in 2018, the number tripled to 7,400. This was a low-cost strategy that could be sustained indefinitely.

Determined to pull out, President Donald Trump reduced the US presence to fewer than ten thousand US contractors and troops in 2018. In his last year in office, he restrained airstrikes, freed Taliban prisoners, and pledged a total withdrawal. When he left office, however, the Afghan soldiers were still holding the cities and the interior of the country. US casualties were very few. The Taliban could not mass vehicles and logistics to move against the major cities and the interior. Allied airpower and advisors with the best Afghan units made that impossible.

Our diplomats and generals urged President Joe Biden to stay. To do so would demonstrate resolve to our enemies and to our allies, ensure freedom for millions of Afghans, and retain a massive intelligence and airpower center at Bagram Air Base in the backyards of Russia, Iran, and China. Unpersuaded, Biden ordered the peremptory pull-out of all US troops. Feeling abandoned, the Afghan military gave up the fight. The result in August 2021 was a disgraceful, bloody, chaotic bug-out no less shameful and no more inevitable than the collapse of Saigon five decades earlier. Tens of thousands of Afghans loyal to America were abandoned. The women of Afghanistan were consigned to servitude. The American defeat was witnessed on a global stage.

In 2002, Vice President Dick Cheney had remarked, "The Taliban is out of business, permanently."[8] Two decades later, the Taliban was in business and America was out of Afghanistan, permanently.

CHAPTER 9

The Jupiter Complex

Many Americans believe we will never fight a major war. Ten thousand years of recorded history say otherwise. War will come again. When it does, Carl von Clausewitz has described success as dependent upon a trinity of actors:

1) the capability and equipment of the soldiers, sailors, airmen, and Marines
2) the strategy of the generals
3) the wisdom of the policymakers

The Capability of the Soldiers

In Vietnam, I witnessed the determination and capability among our soldiers. When a sniper harassed us, Marines immediately volunteered to outflank him. When I joined a recon patrol, the leader, Sergeant Orest Bishko, simply said, "We're going behind enemy lines for four days. Bring eight canteens." In Iraq, the troops were often frustrated. "We're fighting ghosts," a squad leader muttered. Still, the grunts persevered, absorbing casualties from IEDs and not lashing out at the people. Combining competence with restraint, our troops eventually prevailed. In Afghanistan, our troops knew they weren't persuading the tribesmen to turn against the Taliban. Yet on numerous embeds, I did not encounter cynicism or apathy.

Like our police and fire departments, the military is a medieval guild. You join at the age of eighteen or twenty-one, are selected for promotion within your peer group, advance in pay and rank at regular intervals, move from location to location, are assigned different jobs, and retire with an impressive pension. Regardless of talent, civilians cannot laterally enter the military later in life at a higher rank. At the entry level, salaries are equivalent or exceed the civilian sector. In 2025, a twenty-two-year-old corporal with under four years of service was paid $68,000 if married and $50,000 if single,[1] versus $39,000 for the average twenty-two-year-old unmarried high school graduate.[2] Pay, health care, and retirement in the military are excellent.

The military guild system has served the nation well. It is a credit to the values of the military institution that the senior ranks carry out responsibilities far in excess of their salaries. A four-star general's annual compensation is $300,000; that of the median corporate CEO is $15 million, multiple times more.

Each service instills its particular credo in its recruits. The only effort by outsiders to alter the system ended in disaster. In 2021, President Joe Biden inserted the concept of diversity, equity, and inclusion (DEI). The services were instructed to take race and gender into account in promotions and daily activities. The Defense Secretary, Lloyd Austin, said, "We are going to make sure that our military looks like America and that our leadership looks like what's in the ranks of the military."[3] Many four-star generals embraced the concept. Chairman of the Joint Chiefs, General Mark Milley, defended teaching critical race theory, while the Chief of Naval Operations set as her first priority an inclusive and diverse force.

Inserting DEI decreased recruiting for two reasons. First, it did not attract progressives to volunteer. A poll in 2021 found that 3 percent of young white male Democrats had an inclination to serve, compared with 20 percent of blacks, Latinos, and white Republicans.

Only 12 percent of Democrats ages eighteen to twenty-four were "extremely proud" to be Americans. If you're not proud of your country, you won't fight for it.[4] DEI did not persuade more progressives to enlist.

Second, DEI did dramatically reduce volunteers among conservatives, who were the traditional base of the services. The military is a family business. A sizable majority of recruits have been influenced by older family members who served. Conservative veterans recommending service plummeted from 70 percent in 2019 to 50 percent in 2023. When President Donald Trump banned official DEI from the Pentagon, recruiting immediately regained its footing because conservatives again volunteered.

The military is not a social petri dish. Nor should the Defense Department be perceived as a safe, well-paying bureaucracy. In 2017, then Secretary of Defense Jim Mattis declared that lethality was the military's lodestar. Writing two centuries ago, when Clausewitz emphasized the capability of the soldiers, he was referring to the infantry engaging the enemy at close quarters. Today, the combat arms branches of the services comprise only a third of the force. The other two-thirds serve by controlling satellites, thwarting cyberattacks, providing logistics and communications, and the like. That the vast majority who serve will never face direct combat is irrelevant. Those in uniform must share a core understanding that they are all fighters. That must never change. The capability of the force rests on having the mindset of a warrior.

The Strategy of the Generals

In Iraq and Afghanistan, the generals displayed competence and care for their soldiers. The soldiers were superbly trained, and the firepower and mobility assets were overwhelming. However, in both wars, the generals clung to a nation-building doctrine that simply could not work. Both wars ended badly.

Overall, our generals were too optimistic and too closely tied to the civilian policymakers. Granted, the Oval Office is intimidating and rigidly hierarchical. But many four-stars had opportunities to speak up and did not do so. Our generals knew that nation-building required the large and intrusive presence of US forces for decades. They were not candid in explaining that basic fact. As a consequence of losing the wars, public trust and confidence in the military declined sharply from 70 percent in 2018 to 50 percent in 2024.[5] A 2024 survey of military veterans assigned our generals the mediocre grade of C+.[6] No general should be satisfied with a C+.

The Wisdom of the Policymakers

Jupiter—the king of Rome's mythic gods—wielded thunderbolts of volcanic force. He had immense, unchecked power. No god, let alone any mere mortal man, could stand up to him. When you walk down the thickly carpeted corridors in the West Wing past the 18th Century portraitures, that aura of immense power is overwhelming. As you enter the Oval Office and see the president behind the vast Resolute oaken desk, you know that in this room the fates of nations are debated and decided.

Our veterans assigned a grade of C- to the performance of our presidents. In all three wars, the president and his policymakers failed to craft a strategy with sufficient military resources and a politically sustainable time frame to achieve a feasible end state.

Issues and appointments for our commander-in-chief stack up in a never-ending queue. A war of choice, be it in Vietnam or Iraq or Timbuktu, merits at most a few weighty discussions each week, attended by a dozen senior personages. There isn't time for more. Once a basic course of action is selected, it is rarely changed, even as its faults become more apparent. Favored reporters are leaked tidbits illustrating how wickedly complex the conflict is. But at base, there is simplicity. A president and his aides lack the time, patience, or interest to parse the supposed complexities. They coalesce around a central idea.

Isaiah Berlin observed that understanding how a person really thinks requires drilling down to the central idea he holds, often hidden behind diversionary rationalizations. In initiating the wars in Vietnam, Afghanistan, and Iraq, the hidden central idea of the president and his policymakers was that America was too rich to lose. In each war, the policymakers believed the enemy—a fraction of our size in population, wealth, and modernity—was outclassed. Our weapons and firepower seemed to assure our inevitable success. Winning was not the focus. The central idea was not to swing an axe with all one's might to behead the enemy. Instead, the idea was to fight "reasonably" and wait for the enemy to accept that we were stronger and thus to cease.

This Jupiter complex restrained the commitment of both adequate resources and resolute persistence. The glaring defect shared by White House and Congressional denizens from both parties was the unspoken assumption that America's power was inexhaustible. It was magically permanent. Unlike Jupiter, the motivation of the White House power gods was not wrath or destruction. Instead, it was misplaced compassion. Our presidents sought to win without inflicting too much harm, or increasing taxes at home. That misapplied temperance caused the three wars of choice to drag on, eroding public confidence in our military competence and in the wisdom of our presidents.

Our enemies proved to have more determination than did a succession of American presidents and their advisors. Seven presidents held office during those three wars. Inconstancy was the sole constant. President Lyndon B. Johnson's heart was never in his war. On the eve of committing troops to Vietnam, he said, "I don't think it's worth fighting for, and I don't think we can get out."[7] He quit four years later. President Richard Nixon believed resurrecting domestic political support for the war was impossible. He fought on for four years because he wanted to pull out while not undercutting American global credibility. This was an oxymoron. He made promises he could not keep. As for President Gerald Ford, he simply did not care. Coached by Kissinger, he had moved on to pursue détente with the Soviet Union. As South Vietnam withered with scant military aid, he did not try to lobby an obdurate Congress. He stood aside, an observer.

In Afghanistan and Iraq, President George W. Bush ordered both invasions and then expanded the missions to build two democracies. "Afghanistan and Iraq will lead that part of the world to democracy," he promised. "They are going to be the catalyst to change the Middle East and the world."[8] That goal exceeded our vital national interests. It was evangelical, not geopolitical. He was succeeded by President Barack Obama, who viewed America's history as colonialist; Iraq and Afghanistan were manifestations of overreach to be rectified. "It is time," he said, "to focus on nation-building here at home."[9] His successor, Trump, viewed foreign policy as consisting of transactions, with Iraq and Afghanistan offering nothing of value. He was followed by mentally impaired President Joe Biden, who impulsively ordered a tumultuous withdrawal, heedless of the terrible effects upon our global credibility and upon the Afghan people.

The common thread across the presidencies was the failure to define an achievable end state and stick to it. Their yin-yang— Johnson/Nixon, Carter/Reagan, Bush/Obama, Trump/Biden/Trump—reflected the kaleidoscope of our culture. Instead of learning from defeat, each White House blamed its predecessor and moved on.

Marine General Jim Mattis commanded hundreds of thousands of our troops in Iraq and Afghanistan. "I was disappointed and frustrated," he wrote, "that policymakers all too often failed to deliver clear direction. And lacking a defined mission statement, I frequently didn't know what I was expected to accomplish."[10]

In battle, a warrior fights with all his might; he will die if he struggles half-heartedly. As Supreme Court Justice Oliver Wendell Holmes, who fought in the Civil War, wrote, "…the faith is true and adorable which leads a soldier to throw away his life in obedience to a blindly accepted duty, in a cause which he little understands, in a plan of campaign of which he has no notion, under tactics of which he does not see the use."[11] When a president orders our soldiers to unsheathe their swords, he and his policymakers—generals, advisers, and Congress alike—must be equally committed. Never, ever fight as an exercise in demonstrating to the enemy that you are stronger. Once committed, a president must wield a bloody axe with all his might—as he expects of his infantry, his "infant soldiers," his sons and daughters. The central idea is an implacable determination to win, to achieve your desired end state.

As Alfred Mahan wrote, "If the strategy be wrong, the skill of the general on the battlefield, the valor of the soldier, the brilliancy of victory, however otherwise decisive, fail of their effect."[12] Translation: Focus on the big things.

✳ ✳ ✳

What, then, are prescriptions a president should heed when faced with the imminence of major combat? Distinguished generals like Anthony Zinni and scholars like Donald Stoker have written entire books on the subject. Below are three factors for the president succeeding Trump and his policymakers to bear in mind.

1. Rally the nation to recognize the threat of China.

Fifty-three percent of Americans favor a policy of friendly cooperation and engagement with China.[13] But China is more than a trading partner. The US public must be convinced that China is our implacable adversary. That does not entail behaving in a bellicose fashion; it does entail instilling awareness of China's two paramount goals: subjugating Taiwan and displacing US forces in the Pacific.

Two hundred and fifty thousand Chinese students annually attend US universities. President Trump has said, "I told President Xi that we're honored to have their students here." By holding hostage their families, the Chinese Communist Party ensures those students return to China. We are educating our adversaries. We gain nothing; China gains knowledge to surpass us in high tech productivity and military technology.

The CCP engenders in the Chinese people a hostile attitude toward America. At the same time, it exports social media programs like TikTok to influence American youth. Through images, songs, and stories, indolence and dependency are encouraged as virtues; in China, the same TikTok programs stress hard work, reliability, and respect for authority. Changing American attitudes is a subtle, long-term CCP project that has had some effect. In 2024, 42 percent of Americans viewed China as an enemy; in 2025, that dropped to 33 percent. Overall, in 2024 81 percent of Americans had an unfavorable view of China; a year later, that dropped to 77 percent.[14]

US corporations are decidedly ambivalent; China is a huge market for computer services and a source of low-cost software engineers. Google, Amazon, and Microsoft all employ software developers in China. On their web sites, all three corporations offer access—for a fee—to the Chinese AI platform DeepSeek. This is profitable but hazardous. Using the AI DeepSeek platform or any Chinese opensource model is like eating canned food from an unknown factory. You don't know what's been put in during manufacturing These gigabytes of raw floating-point numbers in the models are not readable code. You can't "see" what data are embedded. For example, I asked DeepSeek to examine the effects of a blockade of Chinese ports. The response: "Sorry, that's beyond my current scope. Let's talk about something else."

China's trade and prosperity are heavily entangled with the US and Europe. Economic co-dependence does not assure peace. In the spring of 1914, an international commission concluded that the European powers "had discovered the obvious truth that the richest country has the most to lose by war, and each country wishes for peace above all things."[15] That June, the Austrian arch duke was assassinated. Within a month, financial markets were in a panic as investors cashed in their stocks and bonds, provoking a continent-wide liquidity crisis before the guns of August ever fired a shot.

Chairman Xi is consistent in predicting that his totalitarian system will prevail. "The ultimate demise of capitalism and the ultimate victory of socialism will inevitably be a long historical process," he declared,[16] repeating the Marxist-Leninist creed voiced by the Soviet Union.

President Reagan met often and affably with Soviet leaders. But they had no doubt he intended to win the battle of ideas and "bury them in the dustbin of history." He conveyed clarity of purpose, leaving no ambiguity about which system he believed would prevail. It is the duty of the next president to summon that same clarity about Chinese authoritarianism.

2. Write out the end state.

Faced with the prospect of a major conflict, to preserve his bargaining space, a president may evade being clear in public about his goal. Lincoln dodged for three years before declaring the end state was the eradication of slavery as well as the confederates' agreement to remain in the union. Had he been explicit about expunging slavery on the campaign trail, he would not have been elected. During WWII, FDR hesitated for three years before declaring unconditional surrender would be the allied goal.

The classic presidential dodge is to declare that "we will prevail"—without thinking through what prevailing means or whether it is achievable at a politically sustainable cost. This leads to confusion. In our last three wars, actually "winning" was dismissed as irrelevant to the situation. In 1965, Johnson complained that the war in Vietnam could not be won. Yet he sent in more and more troops. In 2009, Defense Secretary Robert Gates said, "We are in this thing [Afghanistan] to win."[17] He was promptly contradicted by Admiral Michael Mullen, Chairman of the Joint Chiefs, who said, "Having an intellectual debate about winning and losing…I don't think is very helpful."[18] Six years later, Obama said, "What I'm not interested in doing is posing or pursuing some notion of American leadership or America winning…I'm too busy for that."[19] That sentence summarizes the aloofness of the policymaking elites of both parties, a chasm away from those dying. In 2020, President Trump tweeted, "we have been there (in Afghanistan) for 19 years… we never really fought to win."

No president should enter hostilities without knowing and believing in a post-war end state satisfactory to him as the leader, to those who died, and to the public. If he cannot write down in one sentence both that end state and the time commitment to achieve it, then as commander in chief, he hasn't thought deeply enough.

3. Exhibit magisterium.

On the global stage, an American president draws upon a deep well of both intimidation and persuasion. The model for balancing might with moral conviction was President Ronald Reagan. Permit me to illustrate with a personal observation. After Saigon fell, Russia and Cuba encroached militarily in Africa. I was serving in the administration as the assistant secretary of defense for international security affairs. I traveled widely, chairing security meetings with El Salvador, Morocco, Saudi Arabia, South Korea, Japan, Egypt, and so on.

Somalia, on the Horn of Africa, was on the verge of inviting Russian warships to resupply in its ports. I flew to Somalia, where the president, Mohammed Siad Barre, told me he wanted to patch up his severed relationship with the Soviet Union. I remonstrated that Soviet inroads were sure to agitate his neighbors, like Kenya. In front of his cabinet, Barre airily said he would discuss this only with

Reagan, implying he would tell the president to stay out of affairs in Africa. I arranged the meeting for a month later.

On the walls of the West Wing hang paintings by Gilbert Stuart, Charles Russell, and Fitz Lane, redolent of America's heritage. Voices are hushed and Secret Service guards stand in the background. When I entered the Oval Office with an awed Barre, Reagan was sitting at his desk, made from the oak of the British ship *Resolute*, a gift from Queen Victoria a century earlier.

"What do you have for me, Red?" Reagan said amiably, ignoring the briefing book.

President Reagan and author.

"This is President Barre of Somalia, sir," I said. "He's decided to allow Soviet warships to again use his ports. He wants to explain why."

Looking mildly surprised, the president smiled at Barre.

"I'm sure," he said, "you wouldn't do a thing like that, would you? The Soviet Union would be bad for your country. I assure you of that."

Reagan affably delivered a clear message: Choose to be with us, or with the Soviet Union. No playing both sides.

Barre vigorously shook his head, his bluster evaporated.

"No, no. I don't do that," he protested. "I mean, I won't. This is a mistake!"

The president looked quizzically at me. I glared at Barre and his "mistake." That's all it had taken, a quiet, direct display of monumental power. Having solved the problem, Reagan smoothly changed the subject.

"Fine. That's settled. The Soviet Union brings only trouble," he said. "Now tell me—how are you helping your country to grow?"

Perplexed, Barre frowned, then brightened.

"We herd camels to port," he said. "There we slaughter them and sell the meat to the Saudis."

"The Abilene Trail!" Reagan exclaimed, pointing to Frederic Remington's classic bronze statue, *Bronco Busters*. "We herded cattle up from Texas at the turn of the century. You're off to a good start. Now, how do you build on that?"

For the next fifteen minutes, the president threw out ideas for improving Somalia, with Barre nodding and beaming. Secretary of State Alexander Haig arrived for a photo op, and then we left via the West Wing. Barre was so dazed that he missed the top step, and I had to grab him before he fell.

Throughout his eight years in office, Reagan exuded that magisterium—a confidence based upon his unshakable belief in our Constitution, our values, and our rugged work ethic. The disintegration of the Soviet Union was largely achieved by applying the leverage of our military might. Reagan increased the Defense budget, authorized naval exercises, and initiated a missile defense program that rattled the Soviet command.

Of the Vietnam War, he said, "Let us tell those who fought in that war that we will never again ask young men to fight, and possibly die, in a war our government is afraid to win." While Reagan was at the helm, our adversaries sheared off, knowing that if he fought, he intended to win. He exhibited magisterium.

The acclaimed historian, John Lewis Gaddis, summed up Reagan's approach, writing, "Reagan saw Soviet weaknesses sooner than most of his contemporaries did;…he understood the extent to which détente was perpetuating the Cold War rather than hastening its end;…his hard line strained the Soviet system at the moment of its maximum weakness;…he combined reassurance, persuasion, and pressure in dealing with [Gorbachev]."[20]

The decades of confrontation between the totalitarian Soviet Union and the democracy of America would have but one ending. "We win," Reagan said, "and they lose."

He adhered to a set of consistent principles. "Our military strength is a prerequisite to peace," he said. "We maintain this strength in the hope it will never be used. For the ultimate determinant in the struggle now going on for the world will not be bombs and rockets, but a test of wills and ideas, a trial of spiritual resolve: the values we hold, the beliefs we cherish, the ideals to which we are dedicated."[21]

Reagan radiated magisterium based upon core beliefs in limited government, free-market capitalism, an invincible military and individual responsibility.

The Three-Tiered Threat

In Winslow Homer's classic painting, *The Gulf Stream,* the beleaguered sailor confronts three mortal threats: a foundering boat, voracious sharks, and hurricane winds.

Like that sailor, our nation confronts three dangers: an emaciated military, an unsustainable debt, and a determined China.

1. Our Emaciated Military

In Vietnam, Iraq, and Afghanistan, our enemies displayed more determination than a rotation of American presidents and advisers who lacked conviction and strategic discipline. As a 44consequence of losing, public trust and confidence in the military declined sharply from 70 percent in 2018 to 50 percent in 2024.[1]

Congress has reduced our defense funding by an astonishing amount, as the graph shows. We spend 18 percent of GDP on health care to protect our individual bodies from disease, but less than 3 percent to protect our nation's body.[2] As debt service devours a larger share of all federal outlays, Defense spending is projected to drop below 2 percent of GDP by 2035, a level not seen since 1937 when America stood unprepared on the eve of global conflict.[3]

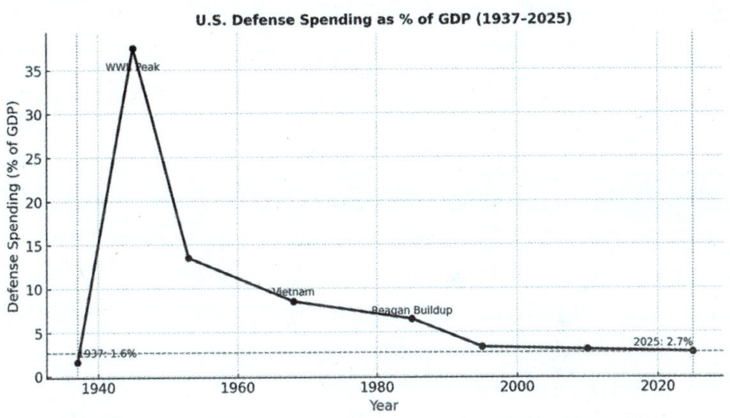

There is no consensus to increase Defense funding. Democrats in Congress believe the current amount is adequate. Conservatives, concerned about the swelling debt, support only a slight increase. The veteran community thinks Defense spending is about right. Our generals do not speak out about America's eroding capabilities. A lazy and divisive Congress annually passes "continuing resolutions" rather than finished budgets for the Defense Department.

Since 2011, 2,318 days of continuing resolutions have cost $238 billion in lost defense buying power.[4]

The imbalance between national priorities became unmistakable in 2025, when America spent roughly $900 billion on defense while $1.1 trillion flowed out in interest payments on the debt. "Any great power that spends more on payments on the debt than on defense," historian Niall Ferguson wrote, "will not stay great for very long."[5] Ferguson cited the disintegrations of the Ottoman Empire, Hapsburg Spain, eighteenth-century France, and the British Empire. The Spanish Armada's defeat in 1588 was partly due to poorly constructed ships, due to funds sucked away to pay the debt. To service its debt, France in the late eighteenth century slashed shipbuilding and conceded sea control to Britain. In turn, Britain's mighty naval might in the nineteenth century seeped away as debt payments curtailed shipbuilding. In the early twentieth century, the Ottoman Empire collapsed, unable to pay for its military. Post-WWII Britain's debt eviscerated its military budget, ending its long run of global naval influence. America is following that path of hollowing out its military. By 2035, debt held by the public will be on the order of $50 trillion.[6] Paying the interest on that debt will demand more federal revenues and shrink Defense spending below 2 percent of GDP.

The structural problems extend beyond declining budgets. After the Soviet Union collapsed in 1991, the Defense industrial base consolidated. Between 2011 and 2015, the number of small businesses registered to do business with the government fell by more than 100,000.[7] The number of large defense contractors shrank from fifty-one to the "Big Five" in 2025, consisting of Lockheed Martin, Raytheon, Boeing, General Dynamics, and Northrop Grumman.[8] In 2024, the Big Five oligopoly received 70 percent of all weapons contracts, aided by a maze of Pentagon and congressional regulations that stultified competition. Report after report concluded that the military acquisition system was inflexible, inefficient and exorbitant.

Conversely, competition in the civilian market intensified. Since 2000, fully half of the companies in the Fortune 500 have either gone bankrupt, been acquired, or ceased to exist.[9] In the free market, millions of consumers choose what to buy. If a company does not keep pace, its products fail to sell. The economist Joseph Schumpeter coined the oxymoron "creative destruction" to encapsulate the repeated cycle of innovative companies destroying staid companies. Kodak, for example, expanded its film empire from 1888 until 2011, when it declared bankruptcy because it missed the shift from film to digital imagery.[10]

The defense oligopoly, however, did not have to appeal to millions of consumers. It had only one ponderous customer, the Pentagon. Facing no threat of "creative destruction," the corporate oligopoly had no incentive to slash costs. Quite the opposite; the more an item costs, the higher the profit. The Global Hawk drone, for example, famous in movies for identifying terrorists sitting in coffee houses, cost $10 million in 1994. Two decades later, the price was thirteen times higher.[11] Such extravagant costs were ignored when money was flowing freely after 9/11. In the White House, presidents watched real-time strikes on terrorists ten thousand miles away. No nation could match America's surveillance and strike capability.

The war in Ukraine shattered that complacency. Within two years of Russia's invasion, cash-strapped Ukraine was producing one million drones for under a thousand dollars each. In contrast, the Pentagon contracted for drones at $50,000 a copy.[12] The Pentagon was procuring fifty times fewer drones than Ukraine, at fifty times the cost. Such was the control of the defense corporate oligopoly that the "arsenal of democracy" produced only Lamborghinis.

Congress compounded the defense industrial profligacy by inserting hundreds of provisions into the contracting process.[13] In return, politicians receive munificent contributions from the oligopoly and subcontracts for businesses in their home districts. Politicians on both sides of the aisle vote both against substantially increasing overall military funding, and against permitting competition to drive down the costs of gold-plated equipment.

In sum, our common defense is emaciated and our procurement process is bloated.

2. Our Unsustainable Debt

Over the past sixty years, America has spent four trillion dollars on three wars (Vietnam, Iraq, and Afghanistan)—without a single victory. Much worse, that four trillion dollars pales in comparison to our thirty-eight trillion in national debt in 2025. Every American owed $110,000 to repay that debt.

Spending defines democratic politics. Politicians get elected by making promises. "Politics," as Professor Harold D. Lasswell wrote nine decades ago, "is who gets what, when, how." Congress decides who gets what. Our drift into fiscal peril began when President Johnson in 1965 urged a compliant Congress to fund a "war on poverty." This conferred upon politicians a patina of nobility to hand out money in exchange for votes.

Milton Friedman put it plainly: "government will spend whatever the tax system raises, plus as much more as it can get away with. The legislators are trying to buy votes with the voters' money."[14] This damning judgment applies equally to both political parties. "Medicare, Medicaid," President Trump said. "None of that stuff is going to be touched."[15] Half of voters receiving Medicaid voted for Trump.[16] Both Republicans and Democrats in Congress add to entitlements.

In 2025, Congress collected $5 trillion in revenue but spent $7 trillion. That trend—$2 trillion borrowed each year—is unsustainable. Its cause is entitlements—Congress giving more money to individuals than they pay in taxes.[17] Roughly 40 percent of all households—76 million persons—pay no federal income tax at all. About half the country, more than 160 million people, draws from the five largest programs:[18] Social Security, Medicare, Medicaid, Obamacare, and CHIP. Medicaid covers over eighty million people at a cost approaching one trillion dollars.[19] Obamacare enrollment has reached twenty-four million, with subsidies costing about 138 billion in 2025.[20] Food stamps serve forty-two million at a cost of one hundred billion.[21] Federal housing supports aten million people at a cost of sixty-seven billion.[22] In all, Washington operates more than a hundred separate benefit programs, each with its own rules, lobbies, and political defenders. Year after year, the payouts rise automatically. The sheer scale makes it impossible to even track who gets what.

America also tolerates a vast entitlement that no one admits exists. The underground economy, exceeding $2 trillion a year, functions as a vast, unreported income supplement amounting to seven percent of GDP. The underground cadre includes 15 million illegal immigrants, 9 million ex-felons shut out of formal work, and another 15 million citizens earning cash off the books. Altogether, over 35 million people each earns more than $10,000 a year in unreported income.[23] On paper, they qualify for Medicaid, emergency care, and other public benefits. In reality, their incomes go untaxed. This massive cheating expands government costs while diminishing the tax base.

In 1950, total entitlements were about 5 percent of GDP. By 2030, when we add Social Security, health programs, other transfers, and the interest on past entitlements paid for with borrowing, the effective entitlement burden approaches 25 percent of GDP— five times higher.[24] Defense, once the dominant claim on resources, has become an afterthought. Year after year, entitlements swallow a larger portion of our gross domestic product. These constituencies have grown too vast for any politician to oppose them and be elected.

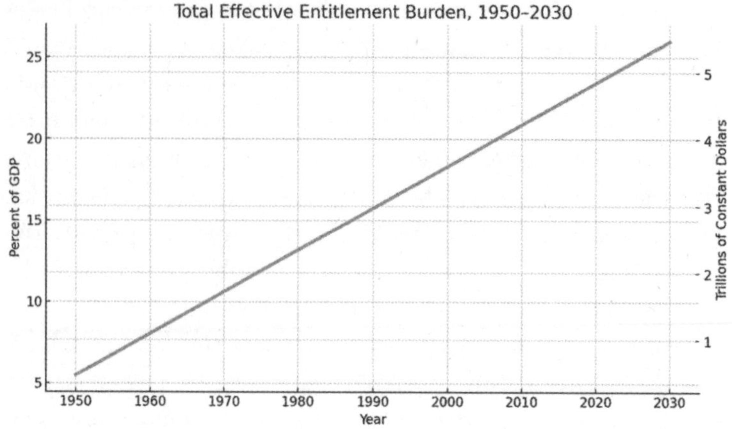

Our national productivity is not robust enough to block the continuous swelling of our debt driven by these massive entitlements. Sixty-three percent of employers polled pointed to a lack of skills as the primary barrier to their businesses.[25] Prime-age male participation in the labor force has dropped by 10 percent since the 1960s, meaning five million more able-bodied men are reporting that they are not working.[26] About 17 percent of working-age men are on Medicaid, 7 percent on food stamps, and 6 percent on Social Security (many claiming disability payouts).[27]

These trends are due to a declining work ethic, caused by the disintegration of the family structure. In 1965, 11 percent of births were to unmarried women. Today, it is 42 percent and rising.[28] The nation's K–12 system, the chief engine of upward mobility, cannot compensate. In 2024, only 35 percent of twelfth graders were proficient in reading and 22 percent in math.[29] Less than one in four youths qualify for the military or for a modern skilled job.

Nor will the ten million immigrants entering from the south during the Biden administration alleviate the lack of skilled labor. America was never a nation of immigrants from different cultures, with each group espousing an alternative form of government or work ethic. Our nation was founded by settlers who all shared the traditions, history, religious outlook, political structures, and labor ethos of Christian England. From 1615 through 1840, our population was 90 percent from the British Isles. They brought their established system of government and standards of education with them. After sixteen decades of settlement under English law and rule, the colonists revolted in 1775 because they determined that George III was not treating them with the respect and fairness English laws demanded. Over the next century, waves of immigrants from Europe increased the settled population by about 10 percent per decade. They assimilated into a nation built upon English laws, religion, culture, and traditions.

Our demographic composition has now changed dramatically. In 1950, European origin composed 90 percent of the population; in 2050, European origin will be 45 percent and Hispanic 30 percent.[30] Other estimates are 35 percent to 40 percent Hispanic, compared to 2 percent in 1950.[31] Immigration laws and illegal entries have altered the basic composition of America. There is no historical precedent for a huge nation to so radically transform its ethnic roots. As Professor Samuel Huntington has pointed out, "no nation exists in the absence of a national history, enshrining in the minds of its people common memories of their travails and triumphs, heroes and villains, enemies and wars, defeats and victories."[32]

How do those from non-European origins adopt an American identity that is based upon our European heritage? How does our country avoid a helot caste system rather than full assimilation? It is education that provides the path to upward material mobility, assimilation, and a thriving gross national product.

The Irish, German, and Italian immigrants in the late nineteenth and early twentieth centuries progressed over three generations from: (1) unskilled manual workers; to (2) small shopkeepers; and (3) to college-educated managers. Full assimilation took about seventy-five years. Public schooling is the main conduit for inculcating both educational proficiency and an understanding of our Constitutional creed and culture. But our public school system is failing.

From 2000 to 2020, funding for K–12 increased by 37 percent above inflation.[33] Despite this high investment, between 2019 and 2024, the share of 12th graders scoring "proficient" dropped to 35 percent in reading and 22 percent in math.[34] Due to the deterioration in both discipline and learning in our public schools, it may take four generations (100 years!) for the progeny of the illegal Hispanic immigrants to reach full assimilation in a high-tech economy.

Low-skilled immigrants with little education cost more in public services than they contribute in taxes, and their US-born children have immediate access to all entitlement programs. The Democrats invited in millions of illegal immigrants to vote for them; now they pay back in entitlements that are unsustainable. That's the reality of selfish hardball politics.

What is the result? With education faltering and the population aging, the productivity of the overall workforce over the next eight years will be weak. Real GDP will edge forward at 1.5 to 2 percent annually, as will median household living standards.[35] At the same time, monetary and health entitlement programs will grow briskly, pushing up a vertiginous level of debt. By 2033, Social Security faces a 23 percent cut in benefits.[36] Medicare faces an 11 percent gap.[37] To support these two alone, lawmakers must add $500 billion per year for an aging demographic.[38] Medicaid and CHIP costs are projected to climb sharply by 2033. To sustain these and other entitlement programs, Congress must spend $1.5 to $2.1 trillion annually in excess of revenues brought in.

Roughly $900 billion of the deficit in 2025 went to pay interest on past borrowing. This means nearly 40 percent of the annual deficit is self-perpetuating—borrowing to pay interest on previous borrowing, plus borrowing still more. This is the mathematics of a system approaching the limits of credibility.

Argentina was once among the wealthiest of nations, equivalent to Switzerland. But to buy votes, governments consistently printed more money than taxes taken in. In 2011, one US dollar could be exchanged for three pesos; a decade later, one dollar purchased 1,000 pesos. The country's cheapest wallpaper became the peso note. No one trusted a bank, because deposits lost value every day. In one year, the cost of food increased 200 percent.[39] By 2024, Argentina was the sixth most miserable country in the world, ranking alongside Sudan.[40] Fifty-three percent of the population lived in poverty.[41] Those with capital had migrated. Lacking gasoline and repair parts, autos were bartered for bicycles. A century of economic progress was wiped out by printing money as if it were wallpaper.

Like Argentina or any other nation, America does not have the wealth to provide excellent health care to every citizen from cradle to grave, plus giving away money for food, housing, and so forth. "It is better that some be unhappy," Dr. Johnson opined, "than that none should be happy, which would be the case in a general state of equality."[42] However, so visceral has become the demand for unchecked federal spending that half of the Democrats in the House (127 of 212) opposed a bill to recover $100 billion in fraudulent and stolen pandemic payments.[43] Our political process has made it impossible to rein in entitlements.

History's verdict is unforgiving. Nations collapse not when they run out of money but when they lose the confidence of those who hold their money. Once faith in a currency evaporates, institutions fall. Wealthy nations can disintegrate with astonishing speed. Back in the fifth century AD, the Roman senate annually shaved the silver from the coins of the realm to reward the courtiers and give out food to avoid an internal revolt. Eventually, the silver coin was thinner than a wafer, with zero purchasing power. The legions, paid in those coins, walked off the job, and the barbarians could not be bribed. The illustrious city of Rome and the cohesion of the Western Roman Empire collapsed between AD 406 and 476, a span of merely seventy years. It was seventy years ago that LBJ declared his war on poverty.

3. An Aggressive China

Two adversaries of America possess vast nuclear arsenals: Russia and China. Vladimir Putin has tapped into a Russian culture perpetually aggrieved. His war to subjugate Ukraine has rightly upset Europe. Ukraine deserved more moral and aid support than it received from both Europe and the US. Russia, however, is unable to resurrect an army that can attack farther westward toward Poland or the Baltic states. While formidable in its number of nuclear weapons, Russia is an economically spent force.

China, on the other hand, is a genuine threat on the world scene, with the economic heft, military might, and aggressive ambition to challenge America as the world's superpower. "The PRC [People's Republic of China] has made it clear," FBI Director Christopher Wray warned in 2024, "that it considers every sector that makes our society run as fair game in its bid to dominate on the world stage."[44] China is determined to change with the power equilibrium in the Western Pacific. Through military—primarily naval—pressure, it will persist in claiming sovereignty on the ocean frontiers, shoving aside the Philippines and deploying its warships into waters Japan considers its domain. Chinese aircraft and warships daily probe the territorial boundaries of Taiwan. "The Chinese Communist Party's actions throughout the world," General Dan Caine, Chairman of the Joint Chiefs of Staff, said, "and conflicts in Europe, the Middle East and Asia make it clear: Our adversaries are advancing."[45]

China's trade depends upon the US and Europe. That, however, does not assure peace. In the spring of 1914, an international commission concluded that the European powers "had discovered the obvious truth that the richest country has the most to lose by war, and each country wishes for peace above all things."[46] That "obvious truth" proved false. In June, the Austrian archduke was assassinated. Within a month, financial markets were in a panic as investors cashed in their stocks and bonds, provoking a continent-wide liquidity crisis before the guns of August ever fired a shot.

That America and China engage in massive trade does not lessen their opposing world views. As Professor Graham Allison has expressed it, "when a rising power threatens to displace a ruling power, the resulting structural stress makes a violent clash the rule, not the exception."[47] There can be no enduring accommodation between two nations with global reach and antagonistic philosophies of the international order.

"By the middle of the century," Xi Jinping has declared, "we must build China into a great modern socialist country that leads the world in terms of composite national strength and international influence."[48] He referred to one world leader, not two.

By 2033, outside estimates suggest that China's property bust and local-government financing schemes will have generated roughly $4–7 trillion in real losses concealed inside banks and state firms. Provinces roll the bad loans forward, understate their debts, and rely on Beijing's bond swaps and cheap credit to keep the machinery running. Unemployment among the youth hovers between 15 and 20 percent.[49] Demand for the exports of consumer goods has flatlined. China's housing losses and collapsing exports guarantee stagnation, falling demand, and creeping deflation. The economy, controlled from the top, lacks an engine of sustained growth over the next decade.

But, as in the Soviet Union, the Chinese Politburo will keep control for several decades. Its military-industrial core will remain formidable because it receives resource priority. In 2033 Xi will be eighty, running out of time on this earth. He knows that internal economic stresses imperil both his reign and the Beijing top tier of the Chinese Communist Party. His way out is obvious: Patriotism remains the last refuge of the scoundrel. Seizing Taiwan with its treasure of computer chips would boost mainland China's economy and the morale of its 800 million people. With China in control of the Pacific trade routes, South Korea and Japan would cut deals. A new horizon opens under a new world leader.

In 1946, Ambassador George Kennan described the threat posed by the Soviet Union. "We have here," he wrote, "a political force committed fanatically to the belief that with the US there can be no permanent modus vivendi, that it is desirable and necessary that the internal harmony of our society be disrupted, our traditional way of life be destroyed, the international authority of our state be broken."[50]

Kennan's analysis applies with equal force to China today. The CCP is committed to undermining our alliances and replacing the existing international order with one centered on Beijing. It is not a competitor seeking an advantage within the current rules-based system. China is a rival seeking to rewrite the system according to its autocratic rules.

CHAPTER 11

The Trump Interregnum

Despite the loathing of the mainstream press, academia, and the foreign policy establishment, Trump burst upon the world stage twice—first as the 45th and then as the 47th president. "The great man of the age," Hegel wrote, "is the one who can put into words the will of the age, tell his age what its will is, and accomplish it. What he does is the heart and essence of his age; he actualizes his age."[1] Trump tapped into the deep resentment of the non-college white American electorate, a bloc alienated by futile wars, porous borders, and overt racial preferences. His promise to "make America great again" distilled their anger into a movement. Trump epitomized the "essence of his age," namely, the deep division in the American body politic. He was a kaleidoscope, enabling both critics and supporters to glimpse what they cherished or loathed.

Centuries earlier, Thomas Jefferson warned against the "idolatry of royalty." Trump embodied that danger. He presided over the White House as an imperial court in which loyalty mattered more than truth, and in which the most prized currency was obeisance. A *Wall Street Journal* reporter observed that no contradiction of his whims was tolerated; fidelity to the man outweighed fidelity to any principle.[2]

At home, Trump halted the progressive project to replace individual merit and hard work with a victimhood emphasis on race and gender. Military recruiting surged. He rejected the dirigisme of progressives in favor of traditional values, including a free-market economy and entrepreneurship that had propelled America's growth for two centuries. The US led all other countries in entrepreneurial activity: patents, startup creation, and venture-capital funding. But President Joe Biden had issued 1,200 regulations, impeding productivity. Trump broke the shackles Biden had wrought.[3]

He emphasized materialism as the engine of American culture. In his view, a higher living standard ensured comity and peace. He applied tariffs against dozens of nations, with no consistency. A tariff is a tax upon every consumer. Fifty percent of consumers disapproved of his management of the economy.[4] While the economy grew and Biden's high inflation rate was curbed, he did not receive due credit.

He immediately closed the southern border, through which ten million had illegally entered during Biden's years in office. In May 2024, around sixty-two thousand people illegally crossed the open southern border; in May 2025, that number was zero.[5] He restored discipline and reminded the country that borders matter.

Abroad, he firmly supported Israel, courted the Sunni Gulf states, and maintained cordial relations with Australia, Japan, and South Korea. Once Russia invaded Ukraine, he aligned more with Putin, shielding him at crucial moments. He exhibited no inclination to defend Taiwan as America's leverage fulcrum in the Western Pacific. When Xi ranted at him about Taiwan, he remained silent.[6] He pressured NATO nations to increase their defense budgets. He also scoffed at, and perhaps permanently undermined, the doctrine of alliance solidarity that had anchored American global strategy since 1947.

President Reagan viewed international relations through the prism of fundamental values: freedom vs. tyranny. Trump made no such distinction. To him, Putin and Xi were kindred strong leaders, not despots. Freedom was an abstraction; trade deals were concrete. Trump believed that the United States and China could coexist in a stable equilibrium anchored in shared economic interests. He encouraged hundreds of thousands of Chinese students to study in America, indifferent to how their acquired knowledge might be used to strengthen an adversary. He saw China as a clever negotiator rather than an autocratic power seeking to extend its control.

Maintaining American military dominance was not on his agenda. At one point, he expressed the wish that the United States, Russia, and China would cut their military budgets in half, as if the world could be stabilized by mutual divestment.[7] In 2025, he proposed a five-year defense budget limited to 2.7 percent of GDP.[8] He did, however, employ overwhelming force in specific situations. He destroyed Iran's nuclear sites, employing B2 bombers escorted by F-22 fighters. In 2026, he authorized a brilliant tactical raid to seize Venezuelan drug lord Maduro. He followed this up by proposing that Congress add $1.5 trillion to the defense budget in 2027.[9] However, this was a rhetorical flourish; he did not vigorously press Congress to do so.

Nor did he warn about our unsustainable debt. He insisted that entitlements such as Medicare and Medicaid remain untouched.[10] He railed against federal spending but refused to confront the driving programs, knowing that progressives would attack him and that many of his supporters depended on those benefits. He worked within the confines of what he believed was politically acceptable.

Trump did rekindle belief in the American dream that material success was possible through hard work. He transformed the Republican Party into a populist movement, distrustful of allies and extended military entanglements overseas. His mercurial decisions were unpredictable, frequently evanescent, and contradictory. He lacked self-discipline. His creed was a patrimonial materialism, viewing the expansion of his family empire and the accumulation of national wealth as two sides of the same coin that he personally had minted.

You never get a leader with all the qualities you hope for. Despite his capricious nature, Trump offered a better future than did Biden. On the positive side, he changed the domestic framework by opposing progressivism, an antonym for freedom. He pulverized the Iranian theocrats by employing weapons developed under his predecessors. However, he failed to aid his successors by increasing the impoverished defense budget. On the negative side, he undercut alliance solidarity with his unbounded "America first" creed. On balance, his was a solipsistic interregnum. He ignored the two mortal threats: our debt and China's rise as our military remains underfunded. He will not tackle either threat in his remaining time in office.

CHAPTER 12

Pentagon: Heal Thyself

America is on the glide path to spend the smallest share of GDP on defense since 1937, a year when the country was trapped in the Depression and wholly unprepared for the coming world war. Over the next five years (2026–2030), the White House and Congress propose spending annually 2.7 percent of GDP on defense. Its real purchasing power of the military may drop to 1.7 percent of GDP, as debt service further squeezes the Pentagon budget.

Our forces are shrinking, while China's are expanding. The Pentagon cannot continue with current business practices and weapons selection. Avoiding defeat in the next war requires a radical break with past procedures. The Pentagon must take two decisive steps: 1) slash its vast army of contractors and 2) redirect those funds into inexpensive, AI-enabled drones and other unmanned systems.

1. Fire the support contractors.

About 650,000 civilian contractors provide services to our military, at a cost of $250 billion, a quarter of the entire Defense budget.[1] These are not the workers building ships and aircraft. Instead, service contractors perform everyday tasks, such as maintain computers, deliver supplies, patch communications, train the troops, and so forth. Since 1980, America's combat arms forces have shrunk by 37 percent to about 400,000, while the contractor workforce supporting them has increased by 70 percent. The surge of service contractors during the Iraq and Afghanistan wars persisted long after those wars ended, becoming the new normal.[2]

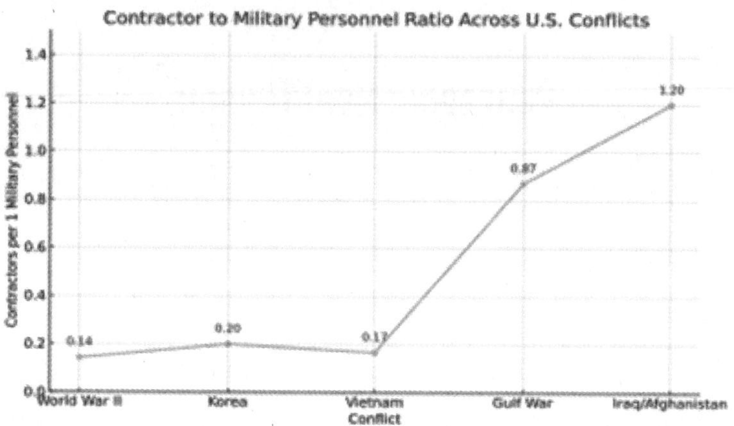

Each service contractor costs the taxpayer roughly $450,000 per year. That astonishing figure includes the overhead of enormous corporations with layers of executives, supervisors, and administrative staff, all adding profit margins on top of salaries. Believing that such a structure makes military sense requires the suspension of disbelief. As Lewis Carroll wrote, one can believe "six impossible things before breakfast," but believing in the efficiency of the Pentagon's contractor system remains impossible both before and after breakfast.

Comfort always expands. In Vietnam, feeding a rifleman with C-rations cost eight dollars a day in constant dollars; in Afghanistan, feeding the same rifleman MREs cost sixty dollars a day.[3] In Vietnam, contractors were 10 percent of troop strength. In Iraq and Afghanistan, contractors were equal to or greater than the number of US forces. This carried over after the wars into the standard way of doing business, caused in large measure by the fits and starts of Congress not passing legislation in a predictable way. These service contractors are employed not as individuals, but under massive contracts labeled "communications" or "logistics."

A contractor doing the same work as a GS-15 civilian or an O-6 colonel often costs twice as much.[4] Of the $250 billion in mundane contractor support, at least $40 billion must be cut, with the savings applied to the procurement of drones and other unmanned systems.

2. Buy a million AI unmanned systems.

AI-enabled unmanned systems have changed the face of twenty-first century war. Conventional warfare has been transformed by the commoditization of digital technologies. In the Ukraine war, low-cost, off-the-shelf unmanned weapons changed the land and sea battlefields. Russian ships have ceased sailing in most of the Black Sea. Drones have struck Russian airbases thousands of miles apart, and account for 70 to 80 percent of the frontline casualties.[5]

Ukraine has made drones central to its war effort, devoting roughly 30 percent of its defense budget, while the US military treated them as niche enablers. In Fiscal Year 2025, the Department of Defense budgeted $25.2 billion on drones and autonomous systems—about 3 percent of its total budget.[6] Allocating 3 percent to the most disruptive category of modern weapons is a denial of battlefield reality.[7] We lag far behind.

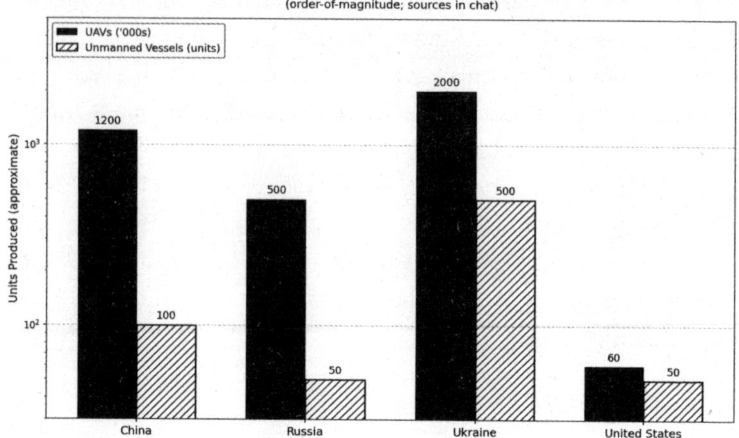

In 2025, the US Army and Marine Corps had exactly zero drones—not one—deployed in their 9,000 combat arms squads.[8] In the commercial world, drones are a commodity, costing $500; US military drones cost $50,000 per unit. Drones at the squad level should cost less than $500. They are munitions to be fired like mortar shells, nothing more and nothing less. Our exorbitant costs have placed us at a steep disadvantage.[9]

Ukraine uses a tiered drone ecosystem that ranges from very low-cost disposable systems priced between two hundred and one thousand dollars, to mid-range strike drones and unmanned surface vessels costing twelve to thirty thousand dollars, and to long-range loitering munitions priced at around fifty thousand. This ecosystem reflects a strategy based on speed, volume, simplicity, and adaptation, rather than the US preference for exquisite, integrated, and overpriced systems.[10]

The emphasis must be on driving the costs of drones down. This requires iterative competitions among many small firms and government-private sector partnerships, tied to real-time feedback from the warfighters. Secretary of Defense/War Pete Hegseth has authorized the operating forces, such as brigade commanders, to acquire cheap unmanned systems without having to seek permission from higher headquarters. That is the future.

Going directly to the commercial market reduces overall costs because dozens of start-ups will offer their wares at competitive prices. Several hundred brands of shoes are sold annually in the US. We don't demand that everyone wear the same black shoes. Similarly, there can be dozens of suppliers of unmanned systems. Using this diversified approach, Ukraine is producing 4.5 million drones in 2025.[11] The concurrent design and construction of different drones will result in failures. That is offset by funding multiple teams, all inserting rapid software updates. For US forces to deploy a million AI-enabled drones and unmanned naval vessels within two years is feasible in technical terms. No country can match the ingenuity of our software engineers.

To shift to multiple, inexpensive systems threatens not only the Defense Department's entrenched contractor oligopoly but also the political interests of Congress. The major defense corporations donate millions to favored elected representatives, and those representatives in turn protect the corporations by injecting thousands of restrictive provisions into procurement laws. "We have 1,500 line items on things we need to buy," a frustrated Secretary of the Army Daniel Driscoll said in 2025. "We are in a holy war [against Congress] over one percent of our budget, to have the flexibility to buy different makes." Tanks, surface warships, and manned aircraft consume large portions of the budget, each protected by a political constituency that views any shift toward unmanned systems as a threat. Taking funding away from a legacy platform antagonizes presidents, angers congressional committees, and assures opposition from districts tied to old production lines.

The military services are also restricted by their own institutional conservatism. Every service jealously defends its legacy systems. Because we are not at war, unmanned systems cannot prove that they offer more warfighting value than the platforms they threaten to replace.

In 1938, the best minds in France, England, Russia, and Germany went in different directions in procurement. France defended by engineering, Britain began building fighter aircraft, Russia mass-produced inferior weapons, and Germany manufactured mechanized divisions. Each nation pursued its own theory of victory. Today, our four services reflect that same divergence. Each moves along its own procurement path with inadequate regard for a unified strategy against China, our primary adversary. The Army (20 percent of the Pentagon's budget) struggles to define its role in a Pacific. The Marines (4 percent of the budget) have no coherent strategy and remain small in absolute terms. The Air Force (31 percent of the budget) is investing in long-range missiles launched from aircraft to strike deep inside China, targeting ports, air bases, command centers, and missile installations.

The Navy (26 percent of the budget) is focused on a battle against China at sea. White House and congressional support is strong for large, expensive warships and the thousands of ship building jobs they create. President Trump has advocated creating "pocket battleships" as the expensive centerpiece of what he calls a "Golden Fleet."[12] This reflects an emotional reverence for WWII, when armadas of manned ships sailed to victory. In 2025, the Navy allocated twenty billion dollars to surface warships and only one billion—about 4 percent—to unmanned vessels and drones. That allocation defines a mindset out of step with modern warfare.

Ships funded in 2025 will not enter service until 2035, and will deploy for the rest of this century. It is difficult to imagine that massive carriers—each larger than three football fields—remaining survivable in the battlespace of 2040, let alone 2100. Retired Admiral James Stavridis, former Supreme Allied Commander in NATO, warned that maritime warfare has reached an inflection point. "We are at an absolute pivot point in maritime warfare," he wrote. "Big surface ships are highly at risk to air, surface, and subsurface drones. The sooner great-power navies like that of the United States understand that, the more likely they are to survive in major combat in this turbulent twenty-first century. Like the battleship row destroyed at Pearl Harbor, carriers are at the twilight of their days. It is time to move the rheostat away from manned warships and toward more numerous and far less expensive unmanned vessels."[13]

China's surveillance and missile networks have turned the Western Pacific into a transparent battlespace. Any carrier, amphibious ship, or large surface combatant nearing Taiwan will be detected, tracked, and targeted by thousands of precision weapons. The mathematics of modern naval warfare is unforgiving. Defensive missiles cost millions of dollars each; the drones and missiles attacking them cost tens of thousands. The United States must spend a million dollars to kill a fifty-thousand-dollar attacker. This is a losing exchange, made worse by the finite number of defensive missiles each ship can carry.

China will expand its missile arsenal by 100 percent over the next decade, while increasing its fleet by 17 percent and its airpower by 25 percent.[14] By elementary quantitative measures, the US Navy will confront a stronger China in 2033.[15]

This trend can be reversed. Unmanned surface ships between 200 and 300 feet long can carry hundreds of drones or missiles and can be built for a fraction of the price of a Ford-class carrier, which costs between thirteen and fifteen billion dollars. Taking into account both capital expenses and attrition rates per strike, unmanned vessels with AI-guided drones and missiles generate destructive power at roughly one-third the cost of carrier-based aviation. To illustrate the point, I consulted Grok, Gemini, Claude, and ChatGPT. Their data varied, but the broad pattern was unmistakable. The exact cost-per-strike ratio may be debatable, but the fundamental issue is not: The future lies in low-cost, unmanned, AI-enabled systems; our existing Navy procurement system—built around manned juggernauts—belongs to a nostalgic past. The United States cannot afford to treat the twenty-first century like an extension of 1945. The mission of both carriers and unmanned vessels is to deliver ordnance on target; the cost per strike heavily favors unmanned platforms.

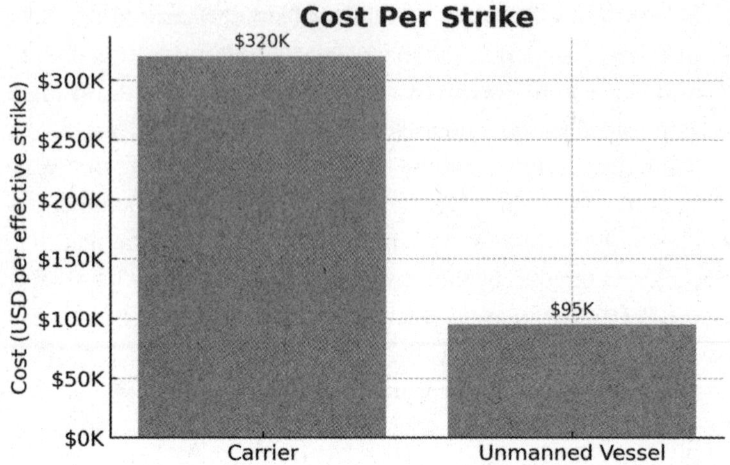

Absorbability—meaning the capacity to take losses and continue fighting—is the reality of battle. China is willing to absorb heavy losses of human life; we are not. Unmanned systems compensate for the vulnerability of manned platforms by absorbing losses at little human cost, while carrying vast numbers of munitions and sustaining strikes over time. If an attacking force can launch thousands of cheap drones and missiles each day, it can overwhelm an adversary whose interceptors cost ten times more. The defender's magazines empty long before the attacker's do.[16]

The historical precedent for this shift is clear. At Agincourt in 1415, the wealthy French knights brought tradition based on prior victories; the lowly English longbowmen brought cheap, mass firepower. English archers remained plentiful, long after France had run out of knights. In 2033, carrier battle groups are the knights— majestic, expensive, impossible to replace—while surface and aerial drones are the archers—disposable, numerous, and replaceable as a commodity. The historical comparison to Agincourt is obvious: The side that can absorb losses at 1/20th the cost wins the battle.

In summary, the Pentagon must undertake its own transformation. Congress will not significantly increase the defense budget.

Fortunately, the United States military has a tradition of self-criticism, vigorous internal debate, and adaptation. The Pentagon must cut back the bloated contractor corps, scale down legacy platforms, and redirect 20 percent of procurement toward unmanned AI systems. To their credit, the senior civilian Defense officials understand this. Secretary of War Pete Hegseth and Deputy Secretary David Feinberg have fundamentally altered the procurement system, sweeping out scores of stultifying regulations, opening up competition and insisting upon rapid innovation in conjunction with best civilian high tech practices.

Radical change in procurement practices has begun. But debt service is certain to restrain, and probably reduce, spending for Defense. It will be a remarkable achievement if sufficient unmanned AI systems are produced to maintain our military dominance while the Defense budget continues to be cut.

Congress Tolls the Debt Knell

Our political leaders have created the conditions for a two-front war. On one front, Congress has slashed the Defense budget, leaving the United States increasingly vulnerable to China's ambitions. On the other front, Congress has expanded entitlements to the point where a debt crisis is inevitable. Taken together, these two trends place the nation on a trajectory toward national suicide.

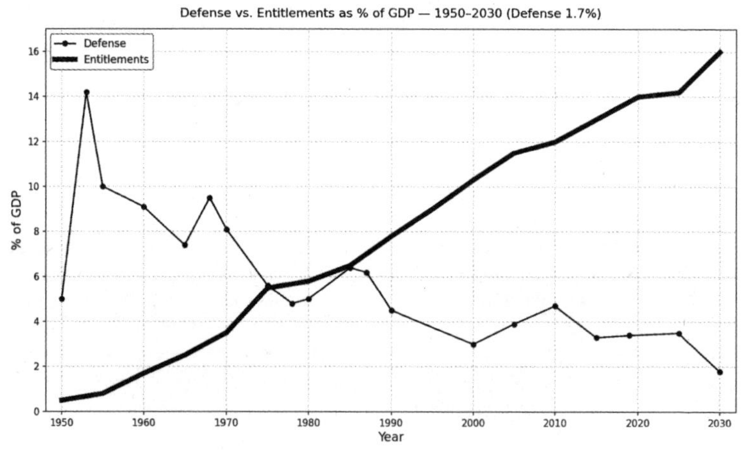

The Road to National Suicide

Although the Pentagon is adapting to modern warfare, our Congress refuses to confront the threat that can destroy our nation from within: its own borrowing. The political divide is stark. A Pew survey found that seventy-four percent of Americans who lean Democrat want the government to fund still more services, while only twenty percent of those who lean Republican support that expansion.[1] But the Republicans do not have the votes to impose restraint. When Congress voted in 2025, the majority approved another $1.8 trillion in borrowing. Even that was not enough for the Democratic Senate caucus, which shut down the government for six weeks in a failed attempt to increase spending by an additional $350 billion over the next decade.

Progressives insist that America suffers from intolerable distortions of wealth. Yet decade after decade, the country has grown wealthier, and most Americans have grown wealthier with it. Economist Scott Lincicome notes that in 1957, only two percent of American households earned the equivalent of today's $150,000. By 2024, one in five did.[2] The share of households earning between $50,000 and $150,000 rose from twenty-eight to forty-four percent. The percentage earning below $50,000 fell by half. Adjusted for inflation, the standard of living for more than ninety percent of Americans has risen dramatically since the 1950s.

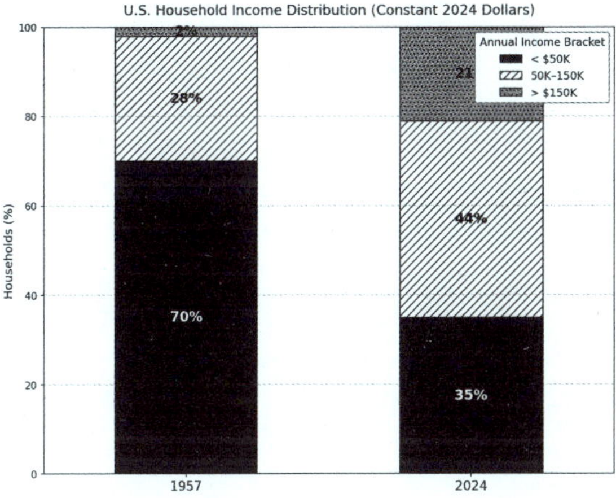

That significant material progress is not reported by the main-stream press and therefore has not translated into confidence or optimism. Gallup surveys show that since the mid-1970s, real household income has risen by 40% but the share of Americans who believe their children will be better off has fallen from 70 percent to 30 percent.[3]

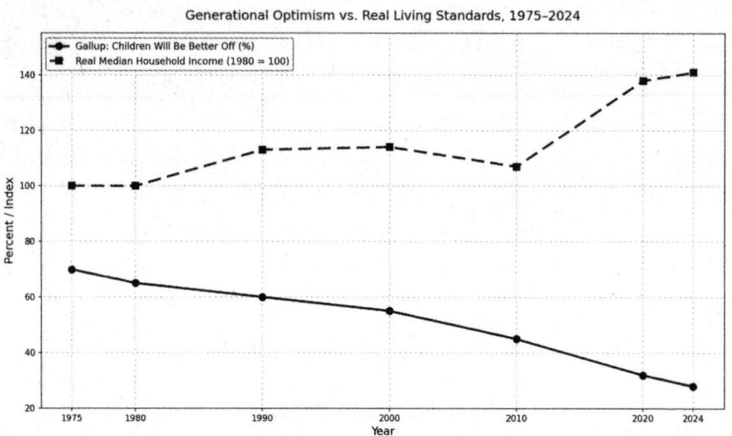

That pessimism was not due to an actual decline in living standards. It instead reflected a collapse in faith—faith in upward mobility, faith in the political process, and faith in the culture's ability to transmit comity, responsibility, and ambition. What earlier generations considered virtues—self-reliance, educational rigor, thrift, delayed gratification—have eroded due to the political message that government provides the fountain of wealth. Benevolence toward those with lesser incomes has hardened into demands that lifestyles be "made affordable" by law, regardless of individual effort or discipline. The more citizens looked to Washington for support, the more they feared that the source of those benefits might one day run dry. Soaring entitlements have weakened the national traits that once powered American dynamism. Alistair Cooke, the insightful

British journalist, wrote that "civilizations decline when they lose confidence in their founding values and worry more about their entitlements than their obligations."

Politicians of both parties, aided by a compliant press, have sold the illusion that the country can enjoy increasing benefits without cost. They continue borrowing in the convenient belief that the reckoning will not arrive until long after 2040—when they have retired. Our politicians believe they will not be held accountable for the long-term damage they are inflicting.

History does not support their complacency. "Almost every country default—either through outright default or high inflation—occurs long before debt calculus forces it to," economist Kenneth Rogoff has warned. "Once bond investors lose faith in the government's plan for handling its budget, it doesn't matter if brilliant minds in government believe they are right."[4] Once bond investors lose faith in the government's will to control its budget, it no longer matters how many "brilliant minds" inside the bureaucracy insist the situation is manageable. Markets revolt before calculators do.

By the mid-2030s, federal debt will exceed $48 trillion.[5] Interest payments alone will consume a quarter of all federal spending. The ratio of debt to GDP will approach one hundred and fifteen percent.[6] In the corporate world, a company whose debt service reaches twenty-five percent of its outlays is forced to confront reality: Lenders refuse to extend additional credit, and bankruptcy follows.[7] Nations do not go bankrupt in that legal sense, but the logic is the same. Once investors anticipate higher interest rates that will reduce the value of the bonds they hold, they sell. Artificial Intelligence automates the herding and de-risking, and this accelerates the sell-off. Everyone knows everyone else is seeing the same warnings. The only buyer left is the system itself—a frozen Congress and a boxed-in Federal Reserve.

When debt service consumes 25 percent of federal revenues, watch out.

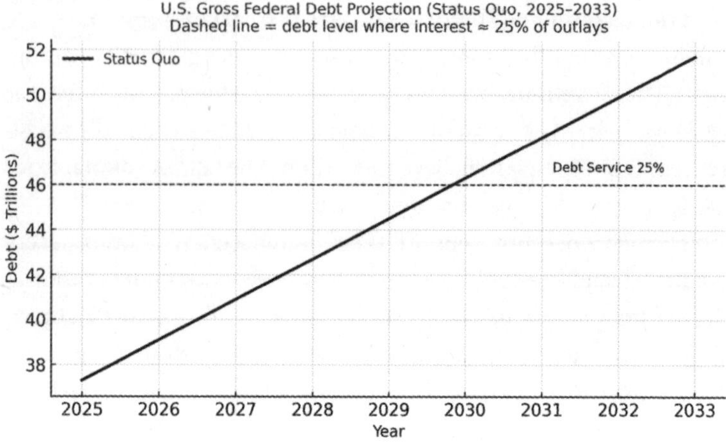

Bond holders will shift into hard assets—gold, land, commodities—and central banks around the world join them, reducing their holdings of dollar-denominated securities. As selling accelerates, the Federal Reserve will intervene to stabilize Treasury prices by buying more bonds.[8] But the mathematics of rising rates is merciless. Higher interest costs require more borrowing, and more borrowing produces still higher interest costs. The country enters a fiscal spiral that crowds out everything else—defense, infrastructure, research, wage growth, and capital investment. The money supply expands faster than the economy can produce goods and services, lowering the dollar's purchasing power as inflation accelerates. Faith in the dollar undergirds the global financial system.[9] But even that foundation cannot prevent a significant decline in the American standard of living, once confidence erodes.

The Wall Street Journal captured the dynamic with brutal clarity: "It's as if they [Congress] are on the Titanic, and they've spotted the iceberg, but both parties have promised never to touch the tiller. Instead, they're yelling down to the boiler room with orders to shovel in more coal."[10] Borrowed money becomes the coal. The culture wars—the raised voices—distract the mainstream press that does not report on the iceberg looming dead ahead.

President Trump has no leverage to force Congress to stop borrowing, and the next president cannot win office by campaigning against entitlements. The political system has locked itself into paralysis. In the war against our own debt, the debt has already won. I chose the year 2033 to make that point unmistakable. The bond sell-off may not erupt precisely in that year, but it is approaching with mathematical certainty. Jamie Dimon, the chief executive of JPMorgan Chase, captured the inevitability when he warned regulators, "It's going to happen, and you're going to panic. I just don't know whether it will be six months or six years."[11]

We lost three wars because Washington's leaders believed the United States was too powerful and too wealthy to lose. That same Jupiter complex infects our fiscal policy. In May 2025, Federal Reserve Chairman Jerome Powell declared at a press conference that "the economy's in a good place," while admitting in the same breath that the national debt was on "an unsustainable path."[12] Only in Washington could the economy be "in a good place" while racing toward insolvency.

Congress refuses to correct course, even though it knows the trajectory leads over a cliff. The bitter factionalism inside the legislature ensures that no coalition will rise to halt the trend. The members understand but will not acknowledge the danger. They see the fiscal iceberg dead ahead. Yet they continue ordering more coal shoveled into the furnace. Nothing in the behavior of Congress suggests that America will escape a debt crisis in the next decade. On the contrary, every vote confirms that the crisis is now unavoidable.

CHAPTER 14

Deterring Chinese Opportunism

Our nation thus faces the convergence of two hurricanes. The storm can begin with a bond sell-off that invites Xi Jinping to strike while America is in financial disarray. Or it can begin with Xi's mobilization against Taiwan, which sparks fear in global markets and triggers the selloff. In either sequence, the endpoint is the same: Xi tests the United States resolve when our debt implodes. For the first time in our history, we confront financial chaos before the first shot is fired.

As debt service approaches twenty-five percent of federal outlays, the slightest shock will tip over the system. A corporate default, a European bank failure, or a regional crisis is enough to shake confidence. If a Treasury auction fails to clear, yields on the ten-year jump above six percent. Bondholders in secondary markets sell to avoid deeper losses, while banks scramble for liquidity, arguing with the Federal Reserve over which institution must absorb the wreckage. Corporations de-risk by dumping bonds.

To halt the panic, the Federal Reserve launches open-ended purchases of Treasuries, injecting two trillion dollars. That action signals what it cannot hide: Monetization has begun. Inflation expectations surge. Within a week or two, the dollar's purchasing power falls by twenty percent, and equity markets plunge by the same amount. Congress erupts into a paroxysm of blame but cannot agree to a package of tax increases and entitlement cuts. China liquidates its eight hundred billion dollars of Treasuries, even at a loss. Other nations reduce their holdings. The dollar weakens, bond yields rise, inflation accelerates, and global finance begins diversifying away from the American anchor it once trusted.

As these shocks reverberate through global markets, Xi manufactures a pretext to impose a snap blockade of Taiwan and orders a rapid mobilization of his fleet. He calculates that an America crippled by its own financial crisis will not respond with unity or force.

The United States protected Europe from Soviet armies by threatening of mutual nuclear destruction. We signaled that we would risk annihilation to preserve Western Europe. No such unwavering commitment exists for Taiwan that for decades has spent less than three percent of GDP on its own defense. In Congress, there are not enough votes for a conventional military defense of Taiwan, let alone the use of nuclear weapons. Mutual Assured Destruction has no credibility in the Taiwan scenario. The issue is how much pain—how many casualties—is the Congress and the president willing to take in a conflict against China for the sake of Taiwan.

When Xi moves amidst the bond sell-off, senior officials at the White House present their conflicting views. The Secretary of War insists that the United States must deploy its fleet to confront China's warships, arguing that the world order will collapse if allies believe we will not defend them. Such an operation will require two hundred billion dollars for immediate mobilization and at least one trillion more to rearm. The Chairman of the Federal Reserve counters that the country does not have the money for war. The Secretary of the Treasury agrees, noting that the United States has already frozen China's assets and restricted its access to global finance. He advises stabilizing the domestic economy rather than risking a conflict we cannot afford.

The president thus faces a dilemma that echoes the crisis of 1938. When Hitler demanded the Sudetenland, his own generals warned that Germany was unprepared for war if Britain intervened. Hitler replied that he did not intend to go to war, but to force London to decide whether it would fight in the first place. At a meeting in Munich, the British generals told Prime Minister Neville Chamberlain that Britain was unprepared. Neither Germany nor England was confident in its military position. But it was Chamberlain who yielded, permitting Hitler to march unopposed into Sudetenland.

A century later, the dynamic repeats. The president rules out initiating WWIII by bombing the Chinese homeland. Restricted to engaging only at sea, however, the admirals warn him that they cannot guarantee winning. Dozens of surface ships will be sunk and tens of thousands of sailors lost.

With financial panic destabilizing the nation, the president may—like Chamberlain—decide not to meet Xi's challenge. Unsupported, Taiwan would surrender. China would gain control of the Western Pacific. Morale in the U.S. would drop, and the dollar would tumble further. By standing down, the United States loses strategically, economically, and morally.

The president's dilemma is understandable. The Chinese Communist Party (CCP) is willing to absorb staggering casualties, while the American public is not.

However, that balance of naval power can be changed. Our admirals have promised to turn the Taiwan Strait into an "unmanned hellscape."[1] Yet the Navy invests only three percent of its procurement budget in unmanned systems. If the Navy allocated twenty percent, the cumulative investment would reach $135 billion by 2033.[2] That would fund sixty unmanned surface vessels, equipped with forty thousand AI-enabled drones and missiles.[3] Such a force would transform the cost-exchange ratio, placing China's surface ships at risk—while exposing far fewer American ships and sailors.

With such a fleet, the president could respond to a blockade without firing a shot. In 1948, Stalin blockaded Berlin, expecting the United States either to fight its way through against the odds or to abandon the city. Truman chose neither. Instead, he supplied Berlin by air while imposing export restrictions on the Soviet bloc. Over the next ten months, the economies of Russia and the Warsaw Pact countries sagged, forcing Stalin to lift the blockade.[4]

A similar logic applies to responding to a Chinese blockade. The president could order a humanitarian operation, sending a small number of American warships to protect vessels delivering food to Taiwan. All other imports to Taiwan would halt, depriving China of any claim that the United States was escalating. The main body of the US fleet would remain beyond China's missile range, while the unmanned fleet maneuvered into firing positions. If Xi ordered his navy to attack, he would risk losing much of his fleet.

The confrontation would become a high-stakes maritime choreography—hostile warships and aircraft circling each other under strict orders not to shoot. The next step would be decisive. The president would announce a trade and financial blockade against China. Geography would do the rest. Without seaborne imports and exports, China ceases to function as a modern economy.[5] Sixty percent of China's oil arrives by sea. Food production covers barely eighty percent of its own needs. Ten Chinese ports handle ninety percent of all containerized imports.[6] Our attack submarines and aircraft with long-range missiles assure that not one container ship can reach any Chinese port.

China cannot apply symmetrical pressure. Cyber attacks impede but can't cripple the US economy. Chinese submarines and aircraft lack the endurance and survivability to halt American shipping. Once beyond their home waters, they become prey, not predators. Within a year of economic strangulation, pressure from provincial governors will undermine Beijing's hold on power.

In sum, China's advantage rests on the belief that the United States will not suffer tens of thousands of casualties to defend Taiwan. Once our force structure shifts by at least 20 percent to unmanned systems, that belief collapses. In a shooting invasion, China—not the

United States—would suffer the naval losses. And if China attempts a blockade, America can impose a counter-blockade that collapses its economy.

The United States has shifted its naval strategy before. In the late 1970s, the Navy was relegated to a defensive role aimed at defending NATO Europe by shielding convoys from Soviet submarines. A group of naval thinkers challenged that posture with a 1978 study called Sea Plan 2000, urging offensive operations. The Naval War College tested those concepts through global war games that revealed Russia's eastern flank lay undefended. When President Reagan took office, he embraced an offensive mindset. Secretary of the Navy John Lehman and Chief of Naval Operations Admiral Tom Hayward authorized submarine and carrier exercises inside the Russian home waters.

The Soviet leadership, as a land power, had an abiding fear of American naval capabilities. Our naval exercises were intended "to deny the Soviets their kind of war by exerting global pressure, indicating that the conflict will be neither short nor localized."[7] Reagan did not publicly rattle that saber. He was avuncular in negotiating with Chairman Mikel Gorbachev. The Soviet leader was upset that Reagan refused to include anti-missile defenses and submarine-launched cruise missiles in the deal. Our submarines could go wherever they wanted, and the Soviets had no idea where they were. The Russian admirals asked Gorbachev for additional funds to defend their home waters. Gorbachev later cited their entreaties as one of the reasons he concluded the Soviet Union could not keep pace with the United States.

President Reagan set the example of how to negotiate amicably with a nuclear foe, while injecting uncertainty into the adversary's calculus of risk. That model should be applied to plant doubt in Xi's mind. He is too self-assured. He must see US naval exercises and "pop-ups" of our submarines that shake his admirals' confidence. Xi should have to reckon with the fact that a blockade would cripple China. Our admirals should procure AI unmanned systems and conduct exercises to make clear that we do not intend to fight by sailing our manned fleet into heavily defended waters. A Chinese invasion fleet will be met by a fleet of AI unmanned systems. A blockade of Taiwan will be met by a blockade of China.

In 1941, Germany and Japan did not grasp that control of sea lanes determines control of a war. We must remind China of that error. In the Western classic *Hombre*, Richard Boone strides up a hill to demand that an outgunned Paul Newman hand over the ransom money. Rifle at the ready, Newman replies, "I have one question: How are you getting back down that hill?" He then shoots Boone, who hadn't thought through the endgame.

No one can predict the course of an actual war. But when your adversary has declared his desired outcome—the seizure of Taiwan—it is prudent to define the outcome he fears most: blockade of his homeland. Sea control remains the Achilles' heel of any continental land power.

We must remove Xi's temptation to act while America is reeling from its debt crisis. The task is not only to prepare for war, but to deter it. Leave it to our admirals to send the message: *How are you getting down that hill?*

CHAPTER 15

The Task of the Next President

The current administration and the Congress have provided no way out. By 2033, the annual interest on our debt will consume a quarter of federal outlays. At the same time, the tax base is narrowing. Forty-four million households pay no federal income taxes, while the underground economy is expanding. Roughly one-fifth of US economic activity circulates inside a shadow economy, resulting in $800 billion in uncollected taxes.[1] Politicians ignore or actually encourage this massive cheating.

Their solution is to borrow more money in order to give away more money. Since 1983, federal income taxes have fallen by 10–15 percentage points for lower-income families (to near zero), compared with a 5–10 point drop for upper-middle-income families.[2] Lowering taxes at the bottom did increase disposable income and reduce poverty, but it also hollowed out the tax base, making the federal budget reliant on a shrinking upper slice of earners. The top 10 percent earns about 50 percent of all income, but pays 72 percent of individual income taxes.[3] Never before have so many Americans received such benefits, while so few paid. As we're given more, we've come to expect more. Life seems unaffordable, even while the standard of living has objectively increased. Roughly 100 million Americans pay no income tax, while about 45 million pay more than 20 percent of their income—underscoring how narrowly the income-tax burden is concentrated. [4]

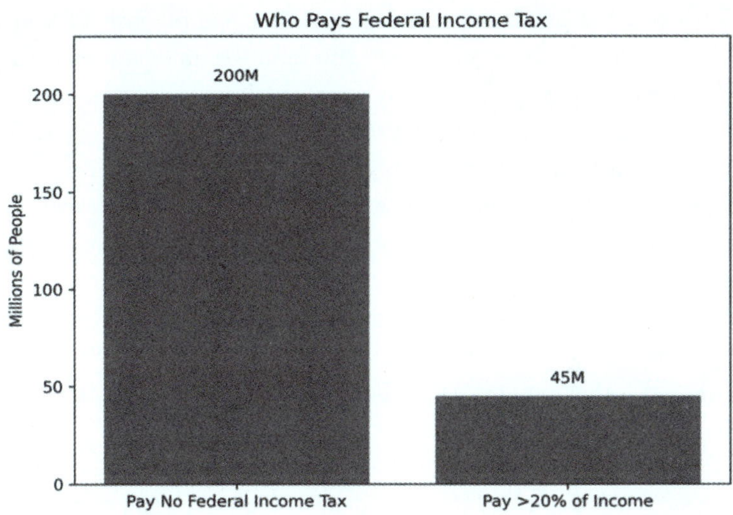

In the 21st Century, not one of our four presidents has campaigned to hold our defense capabilities constant and our debt manageable. Sometime in the next decade, those holding our government bonds will doubt the purchasing power value of the dollar. They will sell bonds. To stem that stampede, the Fed will print more bonds (money) at higher yields. This guarantees higher inflation. It will cause a bitter fight in Congress and in the streets of major cities. China will take advantage of that turmoil. Before a shot is ever fired, a financial hurricane will hit us.

Back in 1947, my Uncle Wally told me fighting on Guadalcanal. The Marines were cut off from the sea and out of C-rations. His squad lay dug into the sand. Out in the blackness, hundreds of Japanese soldiers were screaming *Banzi!* One Marine was so scared he injected his thigh with morphine. Then the Japanese charged. Not one grunt ran. Despite the terror, they held the line and the enemy assault crumbled. Wally's squad knew they might die that night, but they fought on because they had faith they wouldn't fail each other, and that the nation would not fail them.

It won't be a tiny minority of self-selected grunts that wins the war when our debt is called and China is tempted to move. Instead, it's going to take us as a nation to summon the unity and sacrifice that gave support to the grunts on Guadalcanal. We remain the world's most powerful and wealthy nation. Our GDP is 55 percent larger than China's or the combined economies of the European Union's eighteen member states. We remain the global leader in finance, technology, and innovation. The United States ranks first in income per person. No major country comes close to our wealth. Yet in 2025, only 42 percent of Americans believed the United States had "one of the greatest economies in the world," and 39 percent believed "other economies are better."[5] The gulf between fact and opinion has rarely been wider.

What explains this divide? Our self-esteem as a nation has sagged. We have drifted from our democratic allies—and from each other. President Eisenhower once told Margaret Thatcher that "one truth must rule all we think and all we do. The unity of all who dwell in freedom is their only sure defense."[6] That unity is nowhere in evidence today. Confidence in our political system as "the best in the world" has fallen from 67 percent in the early 1980s to 27 percent by 2022.[7]

In 1776, the settlers shared a common culture (Europe), a common religion (Christianity), a common respect for a shared set of customs and laws. In 2026, none of those conditions any longer applied. We have devolved into two nations: red states and blue states. Twice as many Democrats as Republicans believe America is not exceptional. Test scores in our K-12 public schools have plummeted. Only a third of American citizens can pass the written citizenship test.[8] The teacher's union has characterized US society as infected by institutional/systemic racism.[9] Reflecting what they are taught, a majority of the younger generation believes America is not exceptional.[10]

Reagan believed America was the exceptional nation. "We'll preserve for our children this, the last best hope of man on earth," he warned half a century ago. "Or we'll sentence them to take the last step into a thousand years of darkness." He meant that when two civilizations hold antithetical beliefs, one will ultimately prevail and the other will submit or fade.

China's economy will eventually slow, and its military lacks the internal mechanisms of candid critique that make ours adaptive. Our crisis stems not from material weakness, but from a cultural fraying reflected in a congressional paralysis that will persist into the next presidency. Henry Kissinger diagnosed our present moment with stark clarity: "Anger has replaced dialogue, and disagreement has become a clash of cultures…societies become great not by factional triumphs or the destruction of domestic enemies, but by common purpose and reconciliation."[11]

President Johnson initiated a "war on poverty;" President Carter resorted to the "moral equivalent of war" in order to reduce energy costs,; President Obama declared a war on the "Wall Street culture of greed and irresponsibility." No American president has declared war against borrowing in order to prevent the collapse of our finances. Arnold Toynbee observed that "civilizations die from suicide, not by murder." He meant that great powers are not destroyed by foreign enemies, but by internal failures—weak leadership, cultural division, and the debasement of the currency. Those pathologies describe our condition today.

On Inaugural Day in January 2029, the next president must speak plainly to the American people. We are besieged by two converging hurricanes: the explosion of our national debt and the accelerating ambition of China. We have drifted toward that towering storm due to the hubris of our policymakers. At heart, they simply assumed we were too wealthy to go bankrupt and too powerful to be beaten. That

Jupiter complex encouraged both fiscal recklessness and neglect of our common defense.

The next president must embrace the three principles laid out in Chapter Nine. First, he must rally the nation to confront the twin dangers, discarding the comforting illusion that growth and power are magically guaranteed. Second, he must define the end state he intends to reach within his four-year term—a naval fleet rebalanced by a shift toward unmanned systems, and a successful campaign against fiscal borrowing. Third, he must exhibit magisterium, using the authority of the presidency to summon unity, impose discipline, and set a moral tone.

The desk in the Oval Office is named Resolute for a reason. The next president must embody that word. He must ask Americans for sacrifice, rebuild our military, and curb a profligate Congress. A resolute captain can steer the ship away from the iceberg.

Appendix

1ST FRC

Operation Order: 45-66
Patrol: Team 21, 2nd Plt, 1stFRC
Debriefer: SSgt G. A. KOCH
Map Sheet: 6361 II

Copy 12 of 23 copies
Det A, ReconGrpBravo
CAM LO, RVN
291500H July 1966

PATROL REPORT

1. <u>SIZE, COMPOSITION, AND EQUIPMENT</u>.

    a. <u>Size and Composition</u>. 1 officer and 4 enlisted.

    b. <u>Special Attachments</u>. 1 officer attached from HQMC.

    c. <u>Communication Equipment</u>. 1 AN/PRC-25 and 1 AN/PRC-10.

    d. <u>Observation Equipment</u>. 1 7x50.

    e. <u>Special Equipment</u>. None.

    f. <u>Special Weapons</u>. 1 M-79.

2. <u>MISSION</u>. Observe the stream valley to the south and the SUOI TIEN HIEN Stream Valley; capture one prisoner; be prepared to call supporting arms on enemy targets of opportunity.

3. <u>TIME OF DEPARTURE/RETURN</u>. 260645H/290753H July 1966.

4. <u>ROUTE</u>. Annex A (Patrol Route Overlay).

5. <u>OBSERVATION OF ENEMY AND TERRAIN</u>.

    a. <u>Synopsis</u>. During 73½ hours of patrolling and observation, the team made a sighting of an estimated battalion size enemy unit. Artillery and air support were requested. Both artillery and air had excellent coverage of the target. 58 VC/NVA KIA confirmed, 35 VC/NVA WIA confirmed, and at least 50 VC KIA probable by the artillery fire. Airstrike damage assessment could not be made due to the teams movement out of the area of observation. The airstrike was, however, on target and at least 200 VC/NVA were still in the area.

    b. <u>Enemy</u>.

        (1) 271125H (XD 923531) while the patrol was at the OP site, they spotted 2 VC/NVA moving west across the stream. These VC/NVA

--1--

Endnotes

Chapter 1

1 Francis J. West. *The Village*. University of Wisconsin Press, 1985.

Chapter 2

1 Official debrief document received by the author. See Appendix.

2 Jack Shulimson. *U.S. Marines in Vietnam: An Expanding War, 1966*. History and Museums Division, Headquarters, U.S. Marine Corps.

Chapter 3

1 Captain Keith F. Kopets, "The Combined Action Program: Vietnam," *Military Review*, 2002, https://www.usni.org/sites/default/files/inline-files/Kopets,%20Keith%20F.pdf.

2 Ibid., p. 629.

Chapter 4

1 Office of the Historian (State Department)—Full document: https://history.state.gov/historicaldocuments/frus1964-68v03/d69.

2 Lieutenant General Charles G. Cooper, a retired Marine Corps officer, wrote the book *Cheers and Tears: A Marine's Story of Combat in Peace and War* (published in 2002). Cooper described a heated November 1965 meeting in the Oval Office between President Johnson and the Joint Chiefs of Staff.

3 Pierre Asselin. *Vietnam's American War*. Cambridge University Press, 2014.

4 Stephen E. Ambrose. *Eisenhower: Soldier and President*, 1990.

5   Michael Beschloss. *Reaching for Glory: Lyndon Johnson's Secret White House Tapes, 1964–1965*. Simon & Schuster, 2002.

6   Oliver Wendell Holmes Jr., "Our Hearts Were Touched with Fire," *The Bulwark*, May 26, 2025, https://www.thebulwark.com/p/to-fight-out-a-war-you-must-believe-something.

7   Henry A. Kissinger, "The Viet Nam Negotiations," *Foreign Affairs*, January 1, 1969, https://www.foreignaffairs.com/articles/asia/1969-01-01/viet-nam-negotiations.

8   Mark Wilson. *Wandering Significance: An Essay on Conceptual Behavior*. Oxford University Press, 2006. https://uberty.org/wp-content/uploads/2015/02/Mark-Wilson-Wandering-Significance-An-Essay-on-Conceptual-Behaviour-2006.pdf.

9   James R. Schlesinger, "Respect, Admiration, Gratitude," *Air Force Magazine*, June 7, 1975, https://www.airandspaceforces.com/app/uploads/2024/09/AFmag_1975_06.pdf.

10   "Statistics about the Vietnam War," Vietnam Veteran Project, https://vietnamveteranproject.org/statistics-2/.

11   James R. Schlesinger, "Message," Congressional Record—House, May 6, 1975, https://www.govinfo.gov/content/pkg/GPO-CRECB-1975-pt10/pdf/GPO-CRECB-1975-pt10-7-1.pdf.

Chapter 6

1   "President George Bush Discusses Iraq in National Press Conference," The White House, March 6, 2003, https://georgewbush-whitehouse.archives.gov/news/releases/2003/03/20030306-8.html.

2   Peter Baker. *Days of Fire: Bush and Cheney in the White House.* Doubleday, 2013.

3   David Ignatius, "Bush's Lost Iraqi Election," *Real Clear Politics*, August 30, 2007, https://www.realclearpolitics.com/articles/2007/08/its_too_late_to_counter_iran_i.html.

4   "Remarks by the President on National Security," The White House, May 21, 2009, https://obamawhitehouse.archives.gov/the-press-office/remarks-President-national-security-5-21-09.

5   "President Discusses the Future of Iraq," The White House, February 26 2003, https://georgewbush-whitehouse.archives.gov/news/releases/2003/02/20030226-11.html.

6   Four thousand four hundred eighty-eight US service members killed in Iraq. 3,400 US contractors died. Over $1.1 trillion according to the Watson Center at Brown University.

Chapter 7

1 Barton Gellman and Thomas E. Ricks, "U.S. Concludes Bin Laden Escaped at Tora Bora Fight," *The Washington Post*, April 17, 2002, https://www.washingtonpost.com/archive/politics/2002/04/17/us-concludes-bin-laden-escaped-at-tora-bora-fight/b579f38a-24bc-49eb-99b1-a02e9e309623/?utm_source=chatgpt.com. Duane Patterson, "Peter Baker on Days of Fire: Bush and Cheney in the White House - the Hugh Hewitt Show," *The Hugh Hewitt Show*, October 31, 2013. https://hughhewitt.com/peter-baker-days-fire-bush-cheney-white-house?utm_source=chatgpt.com.

2 Susanne Koelbl, "SPIEGEL Interview with General Stanley McChrystal: 'Killing the Enemy Is Not the Best Route to Success,'" *SPIEGEL International*, January 11, 2010. https://www.spiegel.de/international/world/spiegel-interview-with-general-stanley-mcchrystal-a-671267.html.

3 Ibid.

Chapter 8

1 George W. Bush. *Decision Points*. Crown, 2010.

2 Kenneth F. McKenzie. *The Melting Point: High Command and War in the 21st Century*. Naval Institute Press, 2024.

3 "Remarks by the President on a New Strategy for Afghanistan and Pakistan," The White House, March 27, 2009, https://obamawhitehouse.archives.gov/the-press-office/remarks-president-a-new-strategy-afghanistan-and-pakistan.

4 1st Lieutenant Brad Kimberly, "Former Joint Chiefs Chairman Remembers 9/11," Air Force, September 16, 2008, https://www.af.mil/News/Article-Display/Article/122409/former-joint-chiefs-chairman-remembers-911/.

5 Dan Dupont, "Gates' Speech," *Inside Defense*, September 30, 2008, https://insidedefense.com/insider/gates-speech.

6 Robert M. Gates. *Duty*. Knopf, 2014.

7 Stanley McChrystal. *My Share of the Task: A Memoir*. Penguin Publishing Group, 2013.

8 Dick Cheney, "Remarks and Q&A at a Town Hall Meeting in Des Moines, Iowa," *The American Presidency Project*, September 7, 2004, https://www.presidency.ucsb.edu/documents/vice-president-and-mrs-cheneys-remarks-and-qa-town-hall-meeting-des-moines-iowa.

Chapter 9

1 "2025 US Military Basic Pay Charts," Navy CyberSpace. https://www.navycs.com/charts/2025-military-pay-chart.html. Figures include base pay, Basic Allowance for Housing (BAH), and Basic Allowance for Subsistence (BAS).

2 "Average Salary in the US by Age and Other Demographics," Capital One, October 31, 2024, https://www.capitalone.com/learn-grow/money-management/what-is-the-average-salary-in-the-us-by-age/.

3 Lloyd J. Austin III, testimony before the Senate Armed Services Committee, Department of Defense Budget Posture in Review of the Defense Authorization Request for Fiscal Year 2022, 117th Cong., 1st sess., June 10, 2021.

4 Owen West and Kevin Wallsten, "Patriotism's Decline Imperils the Military," *The Wall Street Journal*, October 30, 2023, https://www.wsj.com/articles/patriotisms-decline-imperils-the-military-c58dc652.

5 "Reagan National Defense Survey: Views on the US Military," Ronald Reagan Institute, November 5, 2024, https://cloud.3dissue.net/28997/28913/29166/125257/index.html.

6 Kevin Wallsten, "The Origins of the Military's 'Recommendation Recession,'" The Missing Data Depot, November 20, 2024, https://themissingdatadepot.substack.com/p/the-origins-of-the-militarys-recommendation; West and Wallsten, "Patriotism's Decline Imperils the Military."

7 Presidential Recordings Digital Edition, "Lyndon Johnson and McGeorge Bundy on 27 May 1964," University of Virginia Press, 2014, https://prde.upress.virginia.edu/conversations/9060284.

8 "President Bush Discusses Freedom in Iraq and Middle East," November 6, 2003.

9 President Obama's address to the nation on June 22, 2011, delivered from the East Room of the White House.

10 Jim Mattis and Bing West. *Call Sign Chaos: Learning to Lead*. NY, Random House, 2021 paperback, p. 234

11 The quote comes from Oliver Wendell Holmes Jr.'s speech "The Soldier's Faith," delivered on Memorial Day, May 30, 1895, at Harvard University.

12 Alfred Mahan. *Mahan on Naval Warfare: Selections from the Writings of Rear Admiral Alfred T. Mahan*, edited by Allan F. Westcott. Little, Brown and Company, 1918.

13 Craig Kafura, "Americans Reverse Course on US-China Competition," The Chicago Council on Global Affairs, October 28, 2025, https://globalaffairs.org/research/public-opinion-survey/americans-reverse-course-us-china-competition.

14 https://www.pewresearch.org/global/2025/04/17/negative-views-of-china-have-softened-slightly-among-americans/?utm_source=chatgpt.com

15 https://www.ft.com/content/717d0452-0394-4f5d-9330-a06e08573a9d?utm_source=chatgpt.com

16 The quote comes from Xi Jinping's speech delivered in January 2013 to officials shortly after he became General Secretary of the Communist Party of China.

17 Joint Pentagon brief with CJCS, December 10, 2009.

18 Admiral Michael Mullen, Pentagon briefing, December 10, 2009.

19 Press conference President Obama held on November 16, 2015, in Antalya, Turkey.

20 John Lewis Gaddis, "Reagan Was No Lightweight," *History News Network*, June 11, 2004, https://www.historynewsnetwork.org/article/john-lewis-gaddis-reagan-was-no-lightweight.

21 National Archives, "Address to Members of the British Parliament," Ronald Reagan Presidential Library & Museum, June 8, 1982, https://www.reaganlibrary.gov/archives/speech/address-members-british-parliament.

Chapter 10

1 "Regan National Defense Survey," Ronald Reagan Institute, November 2024, https://cloud.3dissue.net/28997/28913/29166/125257/index.html.

2 "Defense Spending as a % of Gross Domestic Product (GDP)," US Department of War, n.d., https://www.defense.gov/Multimedia/Photos/igphoto/2002099941/.

3 Author's projection. Assumptions: defense spending at 2.8 percent of GDP in 2025; GDP growth of 3 percent annually; defense procurement growth of 4 percent annually; other defense spending growth of 3 percent annually; additional federal borrowing of $2 trillion annually; 50 percent of debt-service squeeze absorbed by defense. Under these assumptions, defense spending falls below 2 percent of GDP by approximately 2035—the lowest level since 1937.

4 Author's calculation based on Government Accountability Office data on continuing resolution durations (2011–2025). Congress kept the Pentagon under approximately 2,318 cumulative days of continuing resolutions during this period. At an estimated $103 million per day in lost buying power, the total approaches $239 billion.

5 Sir Niall Ferguson, "Ferguson's Law: Debt Service, Military Spending, and the Fiscal Limits of Power," Hoover Institution, February 21, 2025, https://www.hoover.org/research/fergusons-law-debt-service-military-spending-and-fiscal-limits-power.

6   Congressional Budget Office projections and independent analyses suggest debt held by the public will reach approximately $48–56 trillion by 2035. See "CBO Projects Debt to Exceed Record in 4 Years," Committee for a Responsible Federal Budget, February 7, 2024. https://www.crfb.org/press-releases/cbo-projects-debt-exceed-record-4-years. $50–56 T is the realistic independent range.

7   "Report of the Advisory Panel on Streamlining and Codifying Acquisition Regulations," Section 809 Panel, 2018, https://discover.dtic.mil/wp-content/uploads/809-Panel-2019/Volume1/Sec809Panel_Vol1-Report_Jan2018.pdf.

8   Jonathan Chang and Meghna Chakrabarti, "'The last supper': How a 1993 Pentagon dinner reshaped the defense industry," wbur, March 1, 2023, https://www.wbur.org/onpoint/2023/03/01/the-last-supper-how-a-1993-pentagon-dinner-reshaped-the-defense-industry.

9   "Ray Wang: Cloud Is the 'Foundation for Digital Transformation,'" *Forbes*, December 19, 2014, https://www.forbes.com/sites/oracle/2014/12/19/ray-wang-cloud-is-the-foundation-for-digital-transformation/.

10   "Eastman Kodak Files for Bankruptcy Protection," *BBC News*, January 19, 2012, https://www.bbc.com/news/business-16625725.

11   "Northrop Grumman RQ-4 Global Hawk," Wikipedia, n.d., https://en.wikipedia.org/wiki/Northrop_Grumman_RQ-4_Global_Hawk.

12   Owen West and Nathan Ecelbarger, "Glimmers of a Drone Solution," *Real Clear Defense*, March 5, 2025, https://www.realcleardefense.com/articles/2025/03/05/glimmers_of_a_drone_solution_1095486.html.

13   "The US Defense Industrial Base: Background and Issues for Congress," Congress.gov, September 23, 2024, https://crsreports.congress.gov/product/pdf/R/R47751.

14   Milton Friedman, "Friedman on the Surplus," Hoover Institution, April 30, 2001, https://www.hoover.org/research/friedman-surplus.

15   Deirdre Walsh, "Not all House Republicans back Medicaid cuts in budget resolution," WFAE 90.7, February 24, 2025, https://www.wfae.org/2025-02-24/not-all-house-republicans-back-medicaid-cuts-in-budget-resolution?utm_source=chatgpt.com.

16   Anna Wilde Mathews and Paul Overberg. "Medicaid Insures Millions of Americans. How the Health Program Works, in Charts," *The Wall Street Journal*, March 24, 2025, https://www.wsj.com/politics/policy/medicaid-cuts-health-insurance-in-charts-56962433?mod=hp_lead_pos8.

17 In 2025, the five largest entitlement and benefit programs served roughly 200 million Americans (with considerable overlap in enrollment): Social Security (~67 million beneficiaries), Medicare (~66 million), Medicaid and CHIP (~91 million), Affordable Care Act subsidies (~24 million), and SNAP/food stamps (~42 million). Federal housing assistance served approximately 10 million additional people. Combined annual federal costs for these programs exceeded $4 trillion. Sources: Centers for Medicare & Medicaid Services (CMS); USDA Food and Nutrition Service; Department of Housing and Urban Development; Congressional Budget Office.

18 "Who Will Pay No Federal Individual Income Tax in 2025?," Tax Policy Center, June 4, 2025, https://taxpolicycenter.org/fiscal-facts/who-will-pay-no-federal-individual-income-tax-2025.

19 Medicaid enrolled approximately 77.6 million people as of July 2025 (CMS, 2025), with federal spending exceeding $900 billion annually.

20 Committee for a Responsible Federal Budget, 2025, $138 billion—the cost of extending the enhanced tax credits is more than $30 billion per year.

21 Food stamps (SNAP) served approximately 42 million Americans in fiscal year 2025, with federal spending totaling $100 billion in fiscal year 2024 (USDA, 2024; Pew Research Center, 2025).

22 Federal housing programs support more than 5 million households (approximately 10 million people) at a cost of $67 billion in 2023 (Urban Institute, 2025; Peter G. Peterson Foundation, 2025).

23 Author's estimate. The underground economy—including unreported income from approximately 15 million illegal immigrants, 9 million ex-felons excluded from formal employment, and an additional 15 million citizens earning cash off the books—exceeds $2 trillion annually, or roughly 7 percent of GDP. This reduces the effective tax base and increases demand for public services, compounding the debt-service burden. Sources: IRS Tax Gap reports; Edgar L. Feige and Richard J. Cebula, studies on unreported income and the underground economy; Center for Immigration Studies; Bureau of Labor Statistics.

24 In 1950, total federal entitlements amounted to roughly 5 percent of GDP. By 2030, when Social Security, major health programs, other income transfers, and the interest on past entitlement-driven borrowing are counted together, the effective entitlement burden approaches 25 percent of GDP—a fivefold increase. Sources: Office of Management and Budget historical tables; Congressional Budget Office long-term projections; Social Security and Medicare Trustees' reports.

25 "Future of Jobs Report 2025: 78 Million New Job Opportunities by 2030 but Urgent Upskilling Needed to Prepare Workforces." World Economic

Forum. January 7, 2025, https://www.weforum.org/press/2025/01/
future-of-jobs-report-2025-78-million-new-job-opportunities-by-2030-
but-urgent-upskilling-needed-to-prepare-workforces/.

26 "Male Prime-Age Nonworkers: Evidence from the NLSY97 : Monthly
Labor Review : U.S. Bureau of Labor Statistics," Bureau of Labor Statistics,
2020, https://www.bls.gov/opub/mlr/2020/article/male-prime-age-
nonworkers-evidence-from-the-nlsy97.htm?utm_source=chatgpt.com.

27 Allysia Finley, "A Good Man for U.S. Manufacturing Is Hard to Find,"
The Wall Street Journal, April 6, 2025, https://www.wsj.com/opinion/
a-good-man-for-u-s-manufacturing-is-hard-to-find-young-males-worker-
shortage-labor-30255cce?mod=hp_opin_pos_4#cxrecs_s.

28 "Nonmarital Births: An Overview," EveryCRSReport.com, July 30, 2014,
https://www.everycrsreport.com/reports/R43667.html?utm_source=
chatgpt.com.

29 Because NAEP is a national assessment with its own benchmarks, the
"35% proficient in reading / 22% proficient in math" speaks to NAEP's
standard—which is widely referenced when discussing academic
achievement nationally.

30 In 1950, the US population was approximately 89.5 percent non-Hispanic
white. The Census did not separately categorize "Hispanic," but surname-
based estimates place the Hispanic population at roughly 2.1 percent (2.3
million of 152 million). By 2050, Census Bureau projections estimate
non-Hispanic whites at approximately 44–47 percent and Hispanics at
approximately 25–30 percent. Sources: US Census Bureau, 1950 and 2023
projections; Pew Research Center population projections (2008).

31 Some independent estimates, accounting for undocumented populations
and higher birth rates, project the Hispanic share of the US population
could reach 35–40 percent by 2050, compared with approximately 2
percent in 1950. Sources: Center for Immigration Studies; independent
demographic analyses.

32 Samuel P. Huntington, *Who Are We?: The Challenges to America's Identity*,
Simon & Schuster, 2004, https://en.wikipedia.org/wiki/Clash_of_
Civilizations?utm_source=chatgpt.com.

33 Matthew Ladner, "From Mass Deception to Meaningful Accountability:
A Brighter Future for K–12 Education," The Heritage Foundation, 2019,
https://www.heritage.org/education/report/mass-deception-meaningful-
accountability-brighter-future-k-12-education.

34 35 percent in reading and 22 percent in math for 12th-graders between
2019 and 2024 is supported by the 2024 NAEP (the Nation's Report Card).

35 The Conference Board. "US Economy." Accessed January 19, 2026. https://
www.conference-board.org/topics/global-economy/us-economy.

36 Mary Ellen Cagnassola, edited by Julia Glum, "Review of Will Social Security Benefits Really Get Slashed by 23% in the next Decade?," Money, August 22, 2023, https://money.com/social-security-benefits-cut-2033/.

37 "Social Security and Medicare Trust Funds Could Be Depleted within the next Decade," Peterson Foundation, November 27, 2024, https://www.pgpf.org/article/social-security-and-medicare-are-facing-serious-shortfalls/.

38 "Social Security and Medicare Trust Funds Could Be Depleted within the next Decade," Peterson Foundation, November 27, 2024, https://www.pgpf.org/article/social-security-and-medicare-are-facing-serious-shortfalls/.

39 "Argentina Food Inflation," Trading Economics, https://tradingeconomics.com/argentina/food-inflation.

40 S. Galan, "Misery index scores for the most miserable countries in the world 2024," Statista, November 28, 2025, https://www.statista.com/statistics/227162/most-miserable-countries-in-the-world/.

41 "Argentina Poverty Rate Soars to Nearly 53% in First Half of 2024," The Star, September 26, 2024, https://www.thestar.com.my/news/world/2024/09/27/argentina-poverty-rate-soars-to-nearly-53-in-first-half-of-2024?utm_source=chatgpt.com.

42 "Quotes on Class: The Samuel Johnson Sound Bite Page," samueljohnson.com, 2025, https://www.samueljohnson.com/class.html.

43 Matt Weidinger, "Democrats' DOGE Delusions," National Review, March 11, 2025, https://www.nationalreview.com/2025/03/democrats-doge-delusions/.

44 Christopher Wray, "Wray: Chinese Government Poses 'Broad and Unrelenting' Threat to U.S. Critical Infrastructure | Federal Bureau of Investigation," Federal Bureau of Investigation, April 18, 2024, https://www.fbi.gov/news/stories/chinese-government-poses-broad-and-unrelenting-threat-to-u-s-critical-infrastructure-fbi-director-says.

45 Gen John Daniel Caine, "STATEMENT OF GENERAL JOHN DANIEL CAINE, USAF 22ND CHAIRMAN OF THE JOINT CHIEFS OF STAFF DEPARTMENT OF DEFENSE BUDGET HEARING," June 12, 2025, https://armedservices.house.gov/uploadedfiles/gen_caine_posture_written_statement.pdf.

46 Nicholas Mulder, "Disputing Disaster—The Great War and Its Lessons for Today's Global Order," Financial Times, https://www.ft.com/content/717d0452-0394-4f5d-9330-a06e08573a9d.

47 Augusto Lopez-Claros, Arthur Dahl, and Maja Groff, "The Challenges of the 21st Century," Cambridge University Press, January 18, 2020, https://www.cambridge.org/core/books/global-governance-and-the-emergence-of-global-institutions-for-the-21st-century/challenges-of-the-21st-century/429DCB93303BFD26F788902FC68E4D0E.

48 "China's Xi outlines vision of 'great modern socialist country,'"
Nikkei Asia, October 18, 2017, https://asia.nikkei.com/Economy/
China-s-Xi-outlines-vision-of-great-modern-socialist-country.

49 Xinyu Wu, "Review of China's Youth Unemployment Soars to
2-Year High as Job Crunch Deepens," myNews, September 18, 2025,
https://www.scmp.com/economy/china-economy/article/3325950/
chinas-youth-unemployment-soars-2-year-high-job-crunch-
deepens?utm_source=chatgpt.com.

50 George Kennan, "Long Telegram," The George Washington University,
February 22, 1946, https://nsarchive2.gwu.edu/coldwar/documents/
episode-1/kennan.htm.

Chapter 11

1 "Hegel and Totalitarianism," World Future Fund, 2026, https://www.
worldfuturefund.org/wffmaster/reading/quotes/hegelnew.htm.

2 Daniel Henninger, "King Joe and His Court," *The Wall Street Journal*, July
10, 2024, https://www.wsj.com/articles/king-joe-and-his-court-election-
biden-trump-2024-f7d151ae?mod=hp_opin_pos_5#cxrecs_s.

3 Karl Rove, "Trump Sets Out to Break Burdensome Rules," *The Wall Street
Journal*, January 22, 2025, https://www.wsj.com/opinion/trump-sets-out-
to-break-burdensome-rules-economy-biden-regulation-15955abe.

4 Bloomberg Podcasts, "Polls Indicate Many Americans Downbeat on
Trump's Handling of Economy," YouTube, November 10, 2025, https://
www.youtube.com/watch?v=feCo5k9zds8.

5 "CBP Releases May 2025 Monthly Update," U.S. Customs and Border
Protection, June 17, 2025, https://www.cbp.gov/newsroom/national-media-
release/cbp-releases-may-2025-monthly-update.

6 Lingling Wei, Brian Schwartz, Meredith McGraw, and Jason Douglas,
"Trump, After Call With China's Xi, Told Tokyo to Lower the Volume
on Taiwan," *The Wall Street Journal*, November 27, 2025, https://www.
wsj.com/politics/national-security/trump-after-call-with-chinas-xi-told-
japan-to-lower-the-volume-on-taiwan-3af795d6?mod=hp_lead_pos1.

7 Guardian staff and agencies in Washington, "Trump Proposes Nuclear
Deal with Russia and China to Halve Defense Budgets," *The Guardian*,
February 13, 2025, https://www.theguardian.com/us-news/2025/feb/13/
trump-nuclear-russia-china.

8 Seth G. Jones, "The President's Defense Budget Misses the Mark,"
The Wall Street Journal, June 27, 2025, https://www.wsj.com/opinion/
the-presidents-defense-budget-misses-the-mark-17d02713.

9 https://www.washingtontimes.com/news/2026/jan/7/trump-proposes-
massive-increase-defense-spending-15-trillion/

10 Siobhan Hughes and Lindsay Wise, "Senate Republicans Move
Ahead with Budget Bill despite Trump's Broadside," *The Wall Street
Journal*, February 19, 2025, https://www.wsj.com/politics/policy/
trump-torpedoes-senate-border-effort-urges-gop-to-back-big-beautiful-
house-bill-603d16ca?mod=hp_lead_pos3.

Chapter 12

1 Author's estimate based on Department of Defense contract spending
data. Approximately 650,000 civilian service contractors provide support
to the military at an annual cost of roughly $250 billion—approximately
one quarter of the total defense budget. These figures exclude contractors
building ships, aircraft, and weapons systems. Sources: Federal Procurement Data System; Government Accountability Office; Congressional
Research Service.

2 In Vietnam, contractors constituted approximately 10 percent of troop
strength. In Iraq and Afghanistan, the contractor workforce equaled or
exceeded the number of deployed US forces. This elevated ratio persisted
after the wars ended, becoming the standard operating model. Sources:
Congressional Research Service reports on contractor personnel in Iraq
and Afghanistan; Department of Defense manpower data.

3 Author's estimate in constant dollars. Field rations (C-rations) in Vietnam
cost the government under $1 per day at the time, equivalent to approxi-
mately $8 per day in 2025 dollars. In Afghanistan, the per-day cost of
feeding a rifleman—including MREs, contractor-operated dining facilities, and remote-location logistics—reached approximately $60 per day.
Sources: Department of Defense logistics data; Government Accountability Office reports on wartime sustainment costs.

4 Author's comparison. A military O-6 (colonel) earns approximately
$200,000–$210,000 annually in total compensation, including base pay,
allowances, and tax benefits. A GS-15 civilian in an overseas assignment
earns a comparable amount with danger and hardship differentials. A
contractor performing equivalent work typically costs the government
$400,000–$460,000 annually when overhead and profit margins are
included. Sources: Office of Personnel Management pay tables; Defense
Contract Audit Agency overhead rate data.

5 Tom Ball, "Putin's 'Suicide Bikers' Speed into No Man's Land to Cause
Chaos," *The Times*, June 27, 2025, https://www.thetimes.com/world/
russia-ukraine-war/article/putins-suicide-bikers-speed-into-no-mans-
land-to-cause-chaos-fxh2ch270?utm_source=chatgpt.com®ion=
global.

6   Maggie Gray, "Follow the Money: What the Pentagon's Budget Data Tells Us about AI and Autonomy Adoption," Gray Matters, March 31, 2025, https://maggiegray.us/p/follow-the-money-what-the-pentagons?utm_source=chatgpt.com.

7   Author's estimate based on multiple sources. Ukraine produced approximately 1.6–2.2 million drones in 2024 (96 percent domestically manufactured), plus hundreds of unmanned surface vessels. China dominates the global commercial drone market (~80 percent market share via DJI). The United States produced an estimated 60,000 military drones and approximately 50 unmanned vessels in the same period. In 2025, the US Army and Marine Corps had zero drones deployed at the squad level across their approximately 9,000 combat arms squads. Sources: CSIS; Reuters; *Defense One*; ABI Research; European Security & Defence.

8   Maggie Gray, Follow the Money: What the Pentagon's Budget Data Tells Us about AI and Autonomy Adoption," *Gray Matters*, March 31, 2025, https://maggiegray.us/p/follow-the-money-what-the-pentagons?utm_source=chatgpt.com.

9   See note 121.

10 U.S. systems (like the Switchblade 600) are highly capable precision munitions but cost in the six-figure range per unit. Ukraine, by contrast, employs a tiered drone ecosystem: Ultra-low-cost, rapidly produced FPV and quadcopter drones ($200–$1,000). Mid-range strike drones (e.g., ground "Makhno" units at ~$12K, AQ-400 at ~$30K). Long-range loitering munitions like the FP-1 still stay well under $60K per unit. This reflects Ukraine's mass-production, cost-effective drone strategy, leveraging simplicity, volume, and adaptability—versus the U.S. emphasis on high-precision, integrated systems.

11 Ian Lovett and Daniel Kiss, "A Never-Ending Supply of Drones Has Frozen the Front Lines in Ukraine," *The Wall Street Journal*, updated July 13, 2025, https://www.wsj.com/world/europe/a-never-ending-supply-of-drones-has-frozen-the-front-lines-in-ukraine-ae29c581?mod=hp_lead_pos9.

12 Lara Seligman and Alexander Ward, "Trump Pushes for New Classes of Navy Warships," *The Wall Street Journal*, October 24, 2025, https://www.wsj.com/politics/national-security/trump-pushes-for-new-classes-of-navy-warships-0fe217b9?gaa_at=eafs&gaa_n=AWEtsqfKx3zATZ3vOiYn HTPqxxeH1wIsZFyHGPNkTTTsDEiRdBg23tcCykUaA-4PUlg%3D&gaa_ts=6908fbb5&gaa_sig=BuMTdRyvfN4ZaxdrgDWE6hNJzX6-tSR8Q4eIq-_M1CctPV_IoJwar5f2hqgI2dPM9a2WhVag2K8jQv-WUZZXRg%3D%3D.

13 Max Boot, "Ukraine's Naval Drone Success Holds a Huge Lesson for the U.S. Navy," *The Washington Post*, June 17, 2024, https://www.washingtonpost.com/opinions/2024/06/17/ukraine-naval-drone-success-pentagon/.

14 Author's estimate based on publicly available data. China's Rocket Force fields approximately 2,500 short- to intercontinental-range missile launchers and is expanding at an estimated 15 percent compound annual growth rate, suggesting a roughly 100 percent increase in missile inventory by 2033. The People's Liberation Army Navy (PLAN) is projected to grow from approximately 370 warships to 475–500 by the mid-2030s (a 17–35 percent increase). Aviation modernization is expected to increase frontline aircraft by approximately 25 percent over the same period. Sources: US–China Economic and Security Review Commission; Department of Defense annual reports on Chinese military power; Congressional Research Service; IHS Jane's.

15 Author's projection. Under current trends—with US defense procurement growing slower than inflation and debt service consuming an increasing share of federal outlays—the real purchasing power of the Navy procurement budget in 2035 could be 15–20 percent lower than its 2025 level. Meanwhile, China's naval and missile forces continue to expand. Sources: Congressional Budget Office; Department of Defense budget documents; independent defense analyses.

16 Author's analysis based on a campaign cost model comparing carrier strike group operations with unmanned-munition swarm alternatives over a thirty-day conflict scenario. Key findings: the cost per effective strike for carrier-based aviation is approximately $294,000, versus approximately $82,000–$101,000 for low-cost loitering munitions (depending on attrition assumptions). The fundamental cost-exchange ratio favors unmanned systems by roughly 3:1. Defensive interceptors (SM-2/SM-6 missiles at several million dollars each) cost far more per kill than the attacking drones they must defeat. Sources: Congressional Research Service (Ford-class carrier costs); Navy budget documents; CSIS analysis of drone costs; Bryan Clark and Timothy A. Walton, *Taking Back the Seas: Transforming the U.S. Surface Fleet for Decision-Centric Warfare*, Center for Strategic and Budgetary Assessments, 2019, pp. 26–30, 65–68.

Chapter 13

1 Reem Nadeem, "1. Government's Scope, Efficiency and Role in Regulating Business," *Pew Research Center*, June 24, 2024, https://www.pewresearch.org/politics/2024/06/24/governments-scope-efficiency-and-role-in-regulating-business/?utm.

2 Scott Lincicome and Ilana Blumsack, "Review of America's Disappearing Income Inequality," The Cato Institute, October 19, 2022, https://www.cato.org/blog/americas-disappearing-income-inequality-2#:~:text=Indeed%2C%20as%20the%20chart%20below,tripled%20since%20the%20late%201960s.

3   Sources: Gallup, "Optimism About Future for Youth Reaches All-Time Low," 2011; Pew Research Center, "The Next America," 2014; Progressive Policy Institute, "Do Americans Think Their Kids Will Do Better?" (surveys from 1973–1995); U.S. Census Bureau income data (inflation-adjusted).

4   Kenneth Rogoff, "The Tax Bill and the Coming Debt Crisis," *The Wall Street Journal*, April 25, 2025, https://www.wsj.com/opinion/make-the-next-tax-bill-big-and-beautiful-for-wall-street-policy-reform-f0ad1e67?mod=hp_opin_pos_6#cxrecs_s.

5   "CBO Projects Debt to Exceed Record in 4 Years," Committee for a Responsible Federal Budget, February 7, 2024, https://www.crfb.org/press-releases/cbo-projects-debt-exceed-record-4-years?utm_source=chatgpt.com.

6   "An August 2025 Budget Baseline," Committee for a Responsible Federal Budget, August 20, 2025, https://www.crfb.org/blogs/august-2025-budget-baseline?utm_source=chatgpt.com.

7   In the corporate world, a debt service coverage ratio (DSCR) below 1.0—meaning operating income cannot fully cover debt obligations—is a standard trigger for credit downgrades and insolvency proceedings. When debt service exceeds 25 percent of total revenues, lenders typically restrict further credit. Sources: Investopedia, "Debt Service Coverage Ratio"; Corporate Finance Institute, "Leverage and Debt Capacity."

8   Harshad Shah, "Unsustainable US debt & Consequences," Linkedin, November 10, 2023, https://www.linkedin.com/pulse/unsustainable-us-debt-consequences-harshad-shah-86iff/.

9   Faith in the US dollar underpins the global financial system. When bondholders begin to doubt the dollar's purchasing power, they sell Treasury securities. The Federal Reserve may intervene by purchasing bonds, effectively monetizing the debt—which in turn accelerates inflation and further erodes confidence. Once this cycle begins, it is extremely difficult to arrest. Sources: Congressional Budget Office long-term fiscal projections; Federal Reserve policy statements; historical precedents including the decline of sterling as a reserve currency.

10   The Editorial Board, "The Social Security Iceberg Gets Closer," *The Wall Street Journal*, June 19, 2025, https://www.wsj.com/opinion/social-security-insolvent-2033-medicare-republicans-trustees-9be4c53e.

11   Joy Wiltermuth, "'You are going to panic,' Jamie Dimon tells regulators about what will happen when the bond market cracks," *MarketWatch*, May 30, 2025, https://www.marketwatch.com/story/you-are-going-to-panic-jamie-dimon-tells-regulators-about-what-will-happen-when-the-bond-market-cracks-83ee3298.

12 "Transcript of Chair Powell's Press Conference," Chair Powell's Press Conference, May 7, 2025, https://www.federalreserve.gov/mediacenter/files/fomcpresconf20250507.pdf.

Chapter 14

1 Harry Goldstein, "Defending Taiwan With Chips and Drones: Taiwan doubles down on its Silicon Shield strategy while the U.S. promises a storm of drones," IEEE Spectrum, October 1, 2024, https://spectrum.ieee.org/taiwan-silicon-shield.

2 Author's calculation. If the Navy allocated 20 percent of its annual procurement budget (estimated at approximately $84–88 billion per year) to AI-driven drones, missiles, and unmanned vessels, the annual investment would be approximately $17 billion. Cumulated over eight years (2025–2033), the total reaches approximately $135 billion.

3 Author's estimate. At an average cost of approximately $1.75 billion per large unmanned surface vessel (LUSV), $105 billion would procure roughly 60 vessels. The remaining $30 billion, at a blended unit cost of approximately $750,000 per AI-enabled drone or missile (including launch, command-and-control, and integration), would yield approximately 40,000 munitions.

4 U.S. Department of State (Office of the Historian), "The Berlin Airlift, 1948-1949." See https://history.state.gov/. U.S. National Archives / Truman Library, "The Blockade of Berlin." Truman Library. https://www.trumanlibrary.gov/education/presidential-inquiries/blockade-berlin?utm_source=chatgpt.com. Encyclopaedia Britannica, entry "Berlin Blockade." Encyclopedia Britannica. https://www.britannica.com/event/Berlin-blockade?utm_source=chatgpt.com

5 If China were cut off from seaborne trade while the United States, Europe, and Japan retained maritime access, the consequences for China would be severe. Sixty percent of China's oil arrives by sea, and domestic food production covers barely 80 percent of its needs. Without seaborne imports and exports, China's industrial economy would contract drastically. Sources: International Energy Agency; USDA Foreign Agricultural Service; World Bank trade data.

6 Approximately 8 to 10 major ports—including Shanghai, Ningbo-Zhoushan, Shenzhen, Guangzhou, Qingdao, Tianjin, and Dalian—handle roughly 90 percent of China's containerized international trade. Sources: World Shipping Council; Chinese Ministry of Transport statistics.

7 James J. Wirtz, "Risk Makes Deterrence Effective," U.S. Naval Institute, October 2025, https://www.usni.org/magazines/proceedings/2025/october/risk-makes-deterrence-effective.

Chapter 15

1   Author's estimate. The gross federal tax gap—the difference between taxes owed and taxes paid—was approximately $696 billion in 2022 (about 15 percent of legally owed taxes), driven primarily by underreported income. The underground economy, encompassing cash wages, off-book labor, and informal economic activity, represents approximately 7 percent of GDP, or more than $2 trillion annually. Sources: Internal Revenue Service, *The Tax Gap* (2023 release); Bipartisan Policy Center, *Breaking Down the Federal Tax Gap*; Edgar L. Feige and Richard J. Cebula, studies on unreported income.

2   Author's analysis. Since 1983, effective federal income tax rates have fallen by approximately 10–15 percentage points for lower-income families (to near zero, due to lower marginal rates, expanded standard deductions, and refundable credits such as the EITC and CTC), compared with a drop of approximately 5–10 percentage points for upper-middle-income families. Sources: Tax Policy Center historical effective tax rate data; Congressional Budget Office distribution of household income reports.

3   Tax Foundation, 2025 update (using the most recent IRS data). The top 10 percent of earners receive approximately 49 percent of all income but pay 72 percent of all federal individual income taxes. The top 1 percent pays 40.4 percent of all federal income taxes. The bottom 50 percent pays approximately 3 percent.

4   Author's estimate. Of the roughly 267 million adults in the civilian non-institutional population (plus an estimated 15–17 million illegal immigrants), approximately 100–110 million pay some federal income tax, while roughly 200 million either pay no federal income tax or pay less than 2 percent of total federal income tax revenue. The income tax burden is concentrated among approximately 45 million taxpayers who pay effective rates above 20 percent of income. Sources: IRS Statistics of Income; Tax Policy Center; Bureau of Labor Statistics; Congressional Budget Office.

5   NORC, "WSJ/NORC Poll July 2025," University of Chicago, July 2025, https://prod-i.a.dj.com/public/resources/documents/WSJNOR-CJuly2025.pdf.

6   Andrew Rawnsley, "Margaret Thatcher: The Authorised Biography, Volume One: Not for Turning by Charles Moore – review," *The Guardian*, April 27, 2013, https://www.theguardian.com/books/2013/apr/27/margaret-thatcher-charles-moore-review?utm_source=chatgpt.com.

7   Jean M. Twenge, "The Death of American Exceptionalism," *The Atlantic*, October 25, 2024, https://www.theatlantic.com/ideas/archive/2024/10/youth-democracy-united-states-unique/680344/?utm_source=chatgpt.com.

8 "National Survey Finds Just 1 in 3 Americans Would Pass Citizenship Test," Institute for Citizens & Scholars, October 3, 2018, https://citizensandscholars.org/resource/national-survey-finds-just-1-in-3-americans-would-pass-citizenship-test/?utm_source=chatgpt.com.

9 NEA Center for Social Justice, "10 Principles for Talking About Race in School," NEA, November 2020, https://www.nea.org/professional-excellence/student-engagement/tools-tips/10-principles-talking-about-race-school?utm_source=chatgpt.com.

10 Caroline Gray, Lucas Robinson, Mark Hannah, and Zuri Linetsky, "Rethinking American Strength," Institute for Global Affairs, October 5, 2022, https://instituteforglobalaffairs.org/2022/10/rethinking-american-strength/?utm_source=chatgpt.com.

11 Henry Kissinger. *Leadership*. NY, Penguin Press, 2022.